HISTORY & GEOGRAPHY 805

A Growing Nation (1820–1855)

INTRODUCTION |3

1. JACKSONIAN ERA 5

SETTING THE TIMES |7
JACKSON'S FIRST ADMINISTRATION |15
THE END OF THE JACKSONIAN ERA |20
SELF TEST 1 |25

2. MANIFEST DESTINY 28

THE NORTHERN BORDER |29
TEXAS AND POLK |34
THE MEXICAN WAR |38
SELF TEST 2 |48

3. GROWTH AND DIVISION 51

THE INDUSTRIAL REVOLUTION |52
CHANGING AMERICAN LIFE |60
THE GREAT DIVIDE |65
SELF TEST 3 |73

LIFEPAC Test is located in the center of the booklet. Please remove before starting the unit.

A Growing Nation (1820–1855) | Unit 5

Author:
Theresa Buskey, B.A., J.D.

Editor:
Alan Christopherson, M.S.

Westover Studios Design Team:
Phillip Pettet, Creative Lead
Teresa Davis, DTP Lead
Nick Castro
Andi Graham
Jerry Wingo

Alpha Omega
PUBLICATIONS

804 N. 2nd Ave. E.
Rock Rapids, IA 51246-1759

© MCMXCIX by Alpha Omega Publications, Inc. All rights reserved.
LIFEPAC is a registered trademark of Alpha Omega Publications, Inc.

All trademarks and/or service marks referenced in this material are the property of their respective owners. Alpha Omega Publications, Inc. makes no claim of ownership to any trademarks and/or service marks other than their own and their affiliates, and makes no claim of affiliation to any companies whose trademarks may be listed in this material, other than their own.

A Growing Nation (1820–1855)

Introduction

1820 to 1855 were turbulent years in American history. Ten different presidents served during those thirty-five years. Only five had served in the first thirty years of the nation. All of the first five presidents except one, John Adams, had served two terms in office. Of the next ten, only one, Andrew Jackson, succeeded in obtaining a second term. The upheaval in the presidency was simply a reflection of the upheaval in the nation.

This was an era of new political parties, expansion, and the rise of sectionalism. The long-ruling Democratic-Republicans fell victim to their own success as they split into factions. Two of these emerged as opposing political parties, the Democrats and the Whigs. The two alternated in control of the government throughout this time period. By 1855, the issue that would not go away, slavery, produced yet another party, the Republicans.

The nation continued to grow at an alarming rate during these years. American immigrants in Spanish/Mexican Texas took over that land and eventually brought it into the Union. A war with Mexico added all of the Southwest and California. Settlements were reached with Britain over Maine and Oregon. A small piece of Mexican land was purchased in 1853 as a railroad route across Arizona and New Mexico. By 1855, all of the land that would create the contiguous 48 states was under U.S. control. Nine new states were added to the nation between 1820 and 1855 as their population grew to reach the required minimum. The natural problems caused by such rapid growth were part of the upheaval of the era.

Slavery and North-South differences were major issues from 1820 to 1855. The country was, at first, divided into three sections: North, South, and West. As the West matured, it joined either the North or South on the slavery issue. Prior to that two-way division, each section had its own agenda and its own representative giant in Washington. Henry Clay from the West, John Calhoun from the South, and Daniel Webster from the North were renowned in their own time for their oratory and their leadership. These men would provide much of the statesmanship that would keep the nation together until after they had died.

Objectives

Read these objectives. The objectives tell you what you will be able to do when you have successfully completed this LIFEPAC. When you have finished this LIFEPAC, you should be able to:

1. Name the leaders of the era and explain their accomplishments.
2. Describe the presidency of Andrew Jackson and its effect on America.
3. Trace the development of the slavery and tariff issues from 1820 to 1855.
4. Define Manifest Destiny and describe its course in America.
5. Describe the course of the Texas Revolution and Mexican War.
6. Define the Industrial Revolution and name the people, innovations, and inventions that contributed to it.
7. Describe the effects of the Industrial Revolution in America.
8. Describe the Second Great Awakening and the reform movements that followed it.
9. Describe the compromises that kept the nation together and what ended them.
10. Describe the changes in America and American life in this era.

A Growing Nation (1820–1855) | Unit 5

Survey the LIFEPAC. Ask yourself some questions about this study and write your questions here.

1. JACKSONIAN ERA

Andrew Jackson's election as president was, like Jefferson's before him, a step in the expansion of democracy in America. The right to vote had been expanding as more and more states dropped property requirements for voters. Jackson, therefore, was elected by the votes of ordinary working people, not the land-owning aristocrats who dominated the voting population a few years before that. His election was a turning point in our history. He was the people's president.

Andrew Jackson was also a man who would shape the government in his own fashion. He had strong opinions and the will, popular support, and party machinery to force them through. He believed he had the support of the people and saw no reason to compromise with Congress or the Supreme Court. His enemies called him "King Andrew I" with good reason. He did exactly what he wanted and changed the face of American government and politics forever.

SECTION OBJECTIVES

Review these objectives. When you have completed this section, you should be able to:

1. Name the leaders of the era and explain their accomplishments.
2. Describe the presidency of Andrew Jackson and its effect on America.
3. Trace the development of the slavery and tariff issues from 1820 to 1855.
9. Describe the compromises that kept the nation together and what ended them.
10. Describe the changes in America and American life in this era.

VOCABULARY

Study these words to enhance your learning success in this section.

abolitionist (ab ō lish' un ist). Person seeking to abolish (end) something, especially slavery.

caucus (kaw' kus). A closed meeting of a group of persons from the same political party to choose a candidate or decide on policy.

censure (sen' chur). An official reprimand.

duel (doo' ul). A formal combat with weapons fought between two persons in the presence of witnesses.

mandate (man' dāt). An authorization to act given to a representative.

nullification (nul i fi kā' shun). The action of a state attempting to prevent the enforcement within its territory of a law of the United States.

Note: *All vocabulary words in this LIFEPAC appear in* **boldface** *print the first time they are used. If you are not sure of the meaning when you are reading, study the definitions given.*

Pronunciation Key: hat, āge, cãre, fär; let, ēqual, tėrm; it, īce; hot, ōpen, ôrder; oil; out; cup, pu̇t, rüle; child; long; thin; /ŦH/ for then; /zh/ for measure; /u/ or /ə/ represents /a/ in about, /e/ in taken, /i/ in pencil, /o/ in lemon, and /u/ in circus.

A Growing Nation (1820–1855) | Unit 5

AMERICA from 1820 to 1855

James Monroe
1817–1825
Democratic-Republican

John Quincy Adams
1825-1829
Democratic-Republican

Andrew Jackson
1829-1837
Democratic

Martin Van Buren
1837-1841
Democratic

William H. Harrison*
1841
Whig

John Tyler
1841-1845
Whig

James K. Polk
1845-1849
Democratic

Zachary Taylor*
1849-1850
Whig

Millard Fillmore
1850-1853
Whig

Franklin Pierce
1853-1857
Democratic

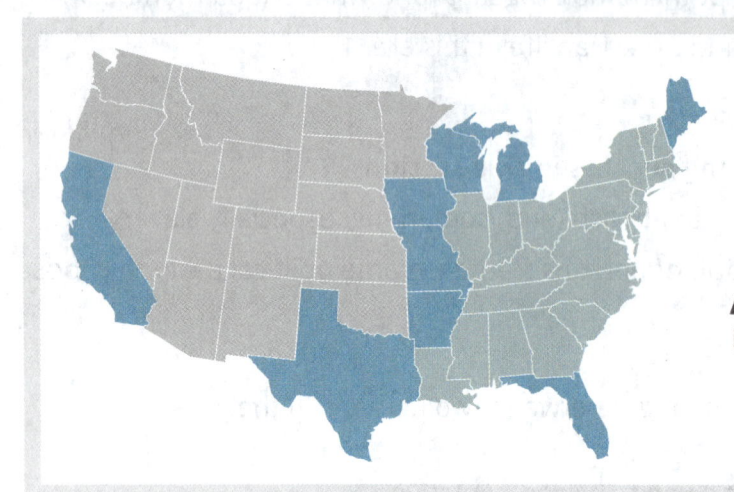

STATES ADMITTED TO THE UNION

Maine	1820		
Missouri	1821	Texas	1845
Arkansas	1836	Iowa	1846
Michigan	1837	Wisconsin	1848
Florida	1845	California	1850

POPULATION of the United States of America

1850 — 23,191,876
1820 — 9,638,453
1790 — 3,929,000

*died while in office

6 | Section 1

Unit 5 | A Growing Nation (1820–1855)

Setting the Times

Giants in Washington. By the beginning of the War of 1812, three men who would be among the most prominent of their era had begun careers in Washington. Henry Clay of Kentucky became a member of the House of Representatives in 1811. He was joined that same year by John Calhoun of South Carolina. They were leaders of the War Hawks who pushed for the war with Britain. Two years later, Daniel Webster of Massachusetts joined the House. These men would serve in Washington in the House, Senate, President's Cabinet, and even the vice presidency until the early 1850s. None of them ever became president, although they all tried. However, no discussion of this era would be complete without an understanding of these men and their influence.

Henry Clay was born in Virginia but moved to Kentucky as a young man to practice law. Clay was a notable speaker and an ambitious, natural leader. He was elected to the House of Representatives, where he often served as the Speaker, and the Senate. He also served one term as secretary of state and ran unsuccessfully for president several times, usually as a Whig. Clay was called the Great Compromiser for his ability to wrangle agreements and resolve crises in the difficult years leading up to the Civil War. He exercised tremendous influence in Congress. He used it to promote programs and compromises to benefit the whole nation. Clay was an ardent nationalist who earned the title of statesman for his work on behalf of the American people.

John Calhoun was born in South Carolina and practiced law there until a wealthy marriage enabled him to concentrate on politics. His federal employment included the House of Representatives, Senate, secretary of war, secretary of state, and vice president. In many ways he reflects the splitting up of the nation that occurred between the Era of Good Feelings and the Civil War. He began his career as a strong Jeffersonian Democratic nationalist.

| Henry Clay, John Calhoun, and Daniel Webster, with their Respective Autographs

He favored a strong federal government and supported Clay's American System to benefit the entire nation. However, as time went on he began to focus more and more on the narrow needs of his own state and region. He opposed the tariffs that protected the northern manufacturers, and became very defensive of the South's "peculiar institution," slavery. In the end, Calhoun became the leading proponent of the doctrine of **nullification** and states' rights. Ironically, he believed this was a way to save the Union by protecting the South. His philosophies became the basis for the Confederacy.

Daniel Webster was born in New Hampshire but moved to Massachusetts as a young man to practice law. He gained tremendous fame as an orator and was one of the best paid attorneys in the nation. He argued and won several key cases before the Supreme Court, including *McCulloch v. Maryland* (states cannot tax the national bank) and *Gibbons v. Ogden* (federal government controls interstate commerce).

A Growing Nation (1820–1855) | Unit 5

He served in the House of Representatives, the Senate, and the cabinet as secretary of state. He was a strong advocate for the manufacturing interests of the North. He opposed slavery, but as a nationalist, he supported compromises on the issue to maintain the Union, something that turned many **abolitionists** against him.

Missouri Compromise. One of the issues that would divide the nation was slavery. It had not been a significant problem when the new Constitution was accepted in 1789. Slavery, although widespread, was not very profitable and might have died on its own had it not been for the cotton gin. Cotton was a popular fiber for cloth, but it was expensive to produce because of the difficulty in separating the fiber from the seeds. In 1793 Eli Whitney invented the cotton gin to help his southern friends. It provided a simple and easy way to separate cotton fiber from the seeds. With the machine, one person could now separate the same amount of cotton that 50 people used to do by hand. Suddenly, cotton production became very profitable.

In the years after 1793, the South concentrated on growing cotton. It purchased its manufactured goods from the North or Europe and its food from the West. Thus, it became completely dependent on cotton for its prosperity. Labor-intensive cotton production, it was believed, depended upon slavery. The institution of slavery, which had been in decline,

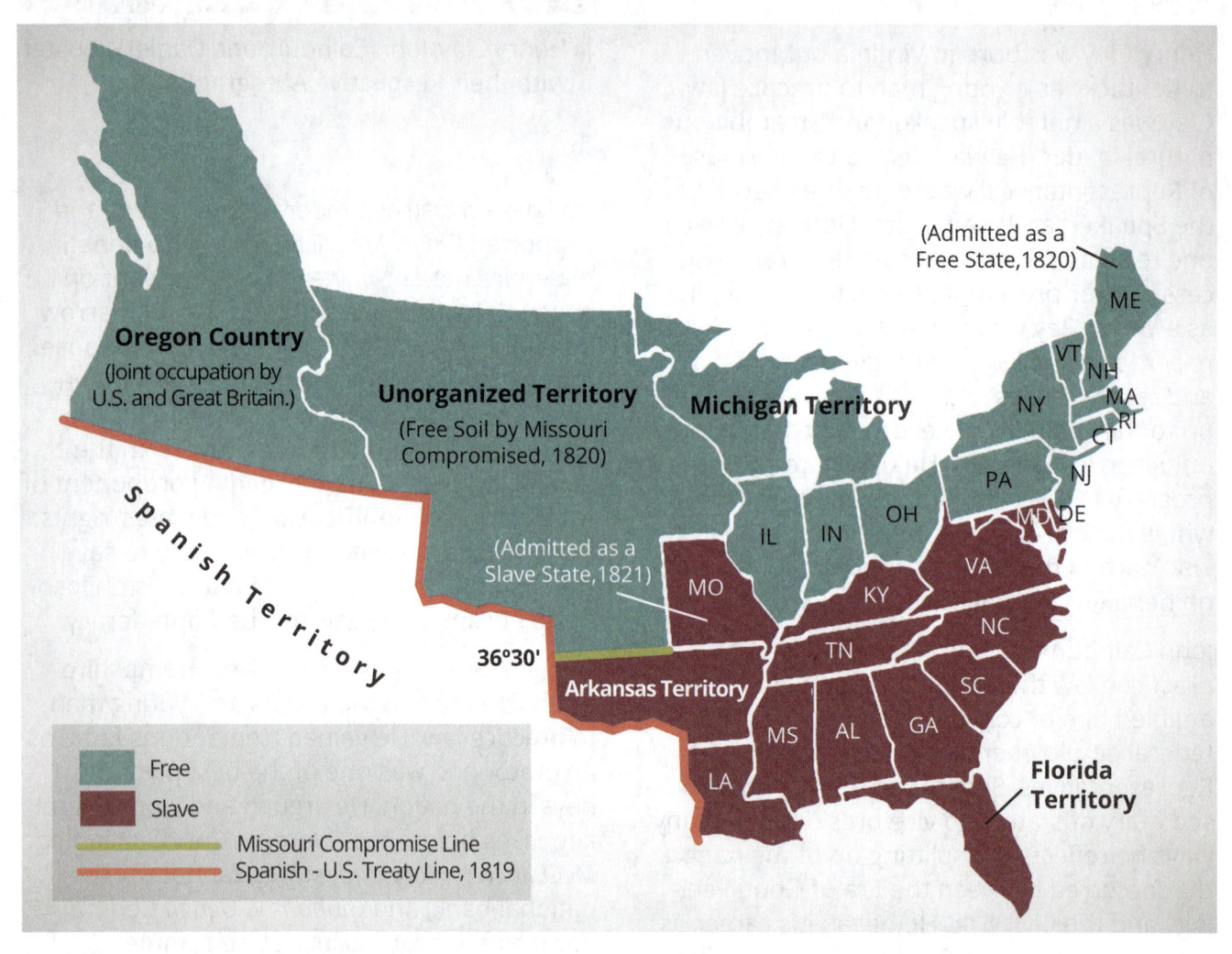

| The Missouri Compromise

rebounded. The South quickly became protective of slavery as the key to their region's wealth and cast a cautious eye to the North and those who opposed it.

The population of the northern states continued to grow in the early 1800s as manufacturing cities provided jobs for more and more people. The South, on the other hand, was stagnant in population. Thus, the North began to significantly outnumber the South in the House of Representatives. However, the slave-holding states were able to protect their interests by controlling half of the Senate. In 1819 the count was 11 slave and 11 free states. That year Missouri asked to be admitted as a slave-holding state.

The North-dominated House of Representatives voted to gradually end slavery in Missouri before admitting it. The South clearly saw the threat. If slavery could not expand with the nation, the slave-holding states would be gradually overwhelmed by the admission of more and more free states. A deadlock occurred that was finally broken by Henry Clay, who led the compromise effort. The result was the Missouri Compromise of 1820. Under its terms, Missouri was admitted as a slave state and Maine, now finally separated from Massachusetts, was admitted as a free state, thereby maintaining the Senate balance. Moreover, slavery was prohibited in all states created in the Louisiana Purchase north of 36° 30' latitude, the southern boundary of Missouri.

The compromise did not solve the slavery issue; it simply kept the political balance between the pro-slave and anti-slave forces. Both sides knew how touchy this issue was and that it might divide the nation. The Missouri Compromise swept the issue of slavery aside for another thirty-five years for the sake of the Union. The North and West continued to grow in size and strength during that time while the moral opposition to slavery also grew. In the end, the issue would have to be faced squarely, but not until the North was stronger.

Tariff Issue. The secondary issue of the South was the tariff. Tariffs raised the price of manufactured goods brought in from abroad. This protected American manufacturers by cutting off cheaper foreign goods. The South, however, had very little manufacturing. All tariffs did was raise the prices they had to pay for things like shoes, farm equipment, and luxury goods. Thus, the tariff became the hot-button issue of the 1820s to 1850s while both sides were avoiding the slavery problem.

A Growing Nation (1820–1855) | Unit 5

Match these people (answers will be used more than once).

1.1 _____ lawyer from Massachusetts
1.2 _____ served as secretary of state
1.3 _____ served as vice president
1.4 _____ invented the cotton gin
1.5 _____ senator from Kentucky
1.6 _____ Speaker of the House
1.7 _____ argued *McCulloch v. Maryland*
1.8 _____ supported states' rights
1.9 _____ nationalist to the end
1.10 _____ ran for president as a Whig
1.11 _____ one of America's highest-paid lawyers
1.12 _____ made cotton production profitable
1.13 _____ strong advocate of manufacturing interests
1.14 _____ Great Compromiser
1.15 _____ senator from South Carolina

a. Henry Clay
b. John Calhoun
c. Eli Whitney
d. Daniel Webster

Answer these questions.

1.16 What were the two issues related to the South?
    a. _____
    b. _____

1.17 What were the terms of the Missouri Compromise?
    a. _____
    b. _____
    c. _____

1.18 What made cotton and slavery suddenly so profitable in the South?
    _____

Election of 1824. The Democratic-Republican party was still the only viable party in 1824, but the unity shown in the unopposed election of James Monroe in 1820 was gone. The tides of change were moving against the stable political powers of Jefferson's party. The first sign was the growing opposition to the nominating procedure. Democratic-Republicans chose their candidate for the presidency in a secret congressional **caucus**. Since there was only one party, the nomination gave the man the office. This process of establishing "King Caucus" was widely denounced in 1824. In fact, the opposition hurt William Crawford who was the official nominee of the caucus that year.

Instead of the united support given to Monroe, the Democratic-Republicans were split four ways in 1824. John Quincy Adams, son of President John Adams, was the candidate of the North. Andrew Jackson and Henry Clay were both candidates from the West. William Crawford was the Southern candidate. Clay and Adams were men of experience with a wide range of government background. Andrew Jackson, the hero of the Battle of New Orleans, had immense popularity all over the country, even if he had fewer qualifications for the job.

Jackson received the largest part of the popular vote (42%), followed by Adams (32%), Crawford (13%), and Clay (13%), whose support in the West had been taken by the popular general. The electoral vote, however, did not give Jackson the majority he needed to become the next president. Under the Constitution, the election had to be decided by the House of Representatives.

Only the top three candidates in the electoral vote could be considered by the House. That left out Clay who had received the lowest count in that crucial vote. Clay, however, was the popular Speaker of the House of Representatives and was in position to influence the outcome of the election. Crawford had suffered a stroke and was unfit to take office, so he was never a factor in the House election. Clay and Jackson had a personal feud that dated back to Jackson's invasion of Florida in the Seminole conflict after the War of 1812. Clay had denounced Jackson in the House for his actions and made himself a bitter enemy. Clay, therefore, chose to support Adams.

John Quincy Adams was elected president by the House on the very first vote because of the influence of Henry Clay. Adams immediately offered Clay the position of secretary of state. This was a prize political plum because it was the office that had launched many of the presidents. Clay unwisely accepted and sealed his own political coffin.

Jackson and his supporters screamed that a deal had been cut trading the presidency to Adams in exchange for the Secretary's position for Clay. It is unlikely that Clay and Adams made an "official" deal for the office. However, the prompt repayment of Adams' political debt to Clay looked corrupt. Jackson and his allies had a ready-made issue for the 1828 election in the "corrupt bargain" between Adams and Clay. Moreover, Jackson was furious that the "will of the people" had been thwarted in such a fashion, and an angry Andrew Jackson was a dangerous opponent.

After the election, the Democratic-Republican Party split. The supporters of Jackson became known as the Democrats, the same party that still exists under that name. The supporters of Adams called themselves the National Republicans and later took the name Whigs, a patriotic name from the Revolutionary War. Andrew Jackson and his Democrats spent the entire four years between the presidential elections building the support they needed to crush Adams and Clay.

John Quincy Adams. John Quincy Adams (1767-1848) was arguably one of the most qualified men ever to assume the presidency. He was extremely honest and hard working. He had seen much of the world traveling with his father as a boy. He was well educated and had written political papers during the early years of the nation. He served his country as a diplomat in Prussia, the Netherlands, Great Britain and Russia. He led the American delegation at Ghent at the end of the War of 1812. He served as a senator from Massachusetts. He also proved to be a highly successful secretary of state under James Monroe. In that position, he created the Monroe Doctrine and negotiated the purchase of Florida from Spain. He also obtained an agreement with Britain for the joint occupation of Oregon and brushed off a Russian attempt to lay claim to the same area.

Adams, however, was not a popular or even very likable man. He had a cold personality, like his father. He had gained his position by ability, not by winning friends and influencing people. He was too honest to make use of public offices to gain support, refusing to throw out hard-working government employees to reward his own people. The "corrupt bargain" also hurt his popular support. His plans for the country were hampered on every turn by his lack of popularity and the violent opposition of the Democrats. His term as president was, therefore, the least notable part of a long and distinguished government career.

In his first address to Congress, Adams proposed an ambitious slate of national improvements including roads, canals, a national university, and an observatory. Americans fighting for survival on the frontier found these intellectual proposals ridiculous! The proposals flew in the face of the rising mood of sectionalism and states' rights. The West and the South in particular had no interest in paying high tariffs for such things. Adam's domestic agenda went nowhere, beat back at every turn by the Democrats. He further alienated the West by trying to control the wild speculation on land and by aiding the Cherokee, who were being evicted from their land by the state of Georgia.

Adams also failed to accomplish anything in foreign affairs, which should have been his best field. Britain's foreign minister, still upset

| "King" Andrew Jackson

over the independent American action with the Monroe Doctrine, refused to discuss removing restrictions on American trade with the British West Indies. Adams and Clay also wanted America to participate in the Panama Congress of 1826, a meeting of the American republics to discuss mutual problems and goals. The Senate took so long to confirm the delegates that the one who survived the trip arrived after the meeting had ended. The incident was an acute embarrassment to Adams.

Tariff of Abominations. Jackson's supporters came up with an unusual way to embarrass Adams during the election year of 1828. They proposed an incredibly high tariff, as high as 45% on some items. Included with it was a tariff on raw materials like wool. The Democrats assumed that New England would be unwilling to accept the tariff on the raw materials they needed for their factories. The tariff bill would therefore fail and cause further problems for Adams in the tariff-hungry North.

The Jacksonians had not counted on just how tariff hungry the North was, however. The tariff passed by a narrow margin and was signed by Adams. The states of the South, particularly the older ones, were furious and called it the "Tariff of Abominations." The old South was the section most affected by the bill because it was the least productive area of the nation. Cotton farming exhausted the soil, and the older farms of the southeastern seaboard were in decline. The rest of the nation did not feel the effects as badly because they were growing and expanding. Thus, the higher prices on goods fell heaviest in the Southern states that had a long tradition of political activism.

The Election of 1828. The election of 1828 brought in a new low in mud-slinging. The need to appeal to the less educated voters brought out a type of campaigning that avoided, rather than stressed, the issues. Adams was accused of purchasing gambling equipment for the White House. (He had bought a billiard table with his own money). He was also accused of drawing excessive salaries during his many government jobs and helping a Russian nobleman get his hands on a pretty servant girl while serving as minister in that nation.

Adams did not engage in any of the wild personal attacks, but his supporters did. Jackson's many **duels** and quarrels were paraded out with embellishments. His mother was accused of being a prostitute. The most serious and painful allegations were charges of adultery and bigamy against Jackson and his wife. According to the official story, Andrew Jackson had unknowingly married his wife, Rachel, before her divorce from her first husband was final. The couple remarried when they found out the divorce had actually been granted almost two years after their first marriage ceremony. The entire episode was very humiliating for Mrs. Jackson, and her husband was furious when it was dragged into the campaign.

The heart of Jackson's campaign was an attack on the "corruption" in Washington, the clearest example being the "corrupt bargain" between Clay and Adams that had given the latter the presidency in 1824. "Jackson and Reform" was the main slogan of the Democrats. Honest, hard-working John Quincy Adams was successfully portrayed in the public mind as the dishonest leader of a gang of corrupt politicians.

Andrew Jackson won both the popular and the electoral vote. He had 178 electoral votes to Adam's 83. Thus, America elected its first president who was not from the old American aristocracy. Jackson was wealthy, but he was a self-made man, a man of the people. The election is sometimes called a revolution because it was the end of the elite that had so effectively run the nation since the Revolutionary War. The power of the vote had reached the masses of the American people, and they chose a man like themselves to run their country.

Adams' Glorious Sunset. John Quincy Adams was not a man to retire into obscurity. He was elected to the House of Representatives and served there with distinction for seventeen years. He earned the affectionate nickname "Old Man Eloquent" for his determination in debates. His greatest achievement was his opposition to the *Gag Rule*. It was a series of resolutions pushed through by the South in 1836 that prevented any petition on slavery from being heard by the House. Adams believed it was an unconstitutional attack on the right to petition. He fought it consistently, trying repeatedly to introduce such petitions until the rule was abolished in 1844. John Quincy Adams collapsed at his desk in the House in February 1848 and, too weak to be removed, died in the Speaker's room two days later.

A Growing Nation (1820–1855) | Unit 5

Check the items that were true of John Quincy Adams.

1.19 ☐ won the election of 1828
1.20 ☐ served as vice president
1.21 ☐ was second in the popular vote in 1824 and 1828
1.22 ☐ was accused of a "corrupt bargain" with William Crawford
1.23 ☐ was capable but not popular
1.24 ☐ won the support of the caucus in 1824
1.25 ☐ served in the House of Representatives after being president
1.26 ☐ wanted to spend government money on national improvements
1.27 ☐ was elected president as a Democratic-Republican
1.28 ☐ was successful in foreign but not domestic affairs as president
1.29 ☐ won the presidency because of Henry Clay
1.30 ☐ was one of three major candidates in 1824
1.31 ☐ led the Panama Congress of 1826
1.32 ☐ was very successful as secretary of state

Answer these questions.

1.33 What was the slogan for Jackson's campaign in 1828?
_____

1.34 What was the tariff of 1828 called?
_____

1.35 Who won the popular vote in 1824?
_____

1.36 What was John Quincy Adams' nickname in the House of Representatives?
_____

1.37 What was the Gag Rule?
_____
_____

1.38 Which of the major candidates was barred from the House election in 1824?
_____

1.39 What were the most serious personal attacks on Jackson in the 1828 campaign?
_____

14 | Section 1

Jackson's First Administration

Andrew Jackson. Andrew Jackson (1767-1845) was one of the most colorful and probably the most violent tempered president our country has ever had. He was born to poor Scotch-Irish immigrants in Carolina in a log cabin. His father died days before he was born. He grew up very wild and mischievous with a limited education. He joined the militia during the Revolution at the age of thirteen. His two brothers and his mother died during that time. Jackson himself was captured and slashed with a sword across the hand and face for refusing to clean a British officer's boots.

Jackson wasted an inheritance from his grandfather in Ireland and eventually took up the practice of law in Tennessee. His fierce attitude and determination in law brought him a measure of success. He made more money by speculating in land and eventually acquired a large plantation named "The Hermitage" near Nashville. He also earned a reputation as a dangerous enemy, fighting constantly over slights to his "honor." Two of his duels left him with bullets in his body for years afterward.

Jackson was a popular man who became well-connected with one of two political cliques that dominated Tennessee. He served without distinction in the House of Representatives and the Senate from 1796 to 1798. He returned to Tennessee and served as a justice of the state's supreme court. His greatest fame was won as the elected general of the state militia in the war with the Creek People and as commander of the U.S. army in the Battle of New Orleans. It was as a militia leader that he won his nickname "Old Hickory" for his toughness.

Old Hickory was wildly popular with the common people of America, especially in the West. He was no eastern aristocrat but a man who, like many on the frontier, had made it on his own in spite of fierce obstacles. He took with him into the White House many of the prejudices of the West, including a hatred of the Native Americans, a distrust of banks, and a determination to expand the nation. He had little respect for the compromise and debate of the democratic process. In fact, he was more comfortable with the command of a general than the leadership of a president. He took the presidency to new heights as he insisted on using the power of the office as he saw fit. He changed the office and the nation.

Inauguration. The extent of the change in Washington could be seen by Jackson's inauguration. It was a wild affair. The president-elect walked to the Capitol to take the oath of office and then to the White House for a reception. All along the route he shook hands and greeted the throngs of people in attendance. The White House reception was thrown open to everyone who wanted to attend. Hundreds of people mobbed the place. They stood on the furniture to get a look at the president. China and glass were broken. Curtains and upholstery ripped. The crush got so heavy that Jackson had to leave to avoid injury! The situation was finally relieved when the staff wisely began serving spiked punch on the lawn. The crowd quickly abandoned the house. One well-heeled Washington resident said it was the rule of "King Mob."

| Crowds at Jackson's Inauguration

Spoils System. Andrew Jackson brought the spoils system to the national government on a large scale. The spoils system was based on the concept, "To the victors go the spoils of the enemy." In this case, it was jobs in the government. Jackson firmly believed in rotation in office, and that in a democracy government jobs should not be held for life. He also believed that he needed to change out the "corrupt" officeholders from the Adams' administration. What he wound up doing was initiating the replacement of government employees with people whose primary qualification was their loyalty to the Democratic cause. In all, he replaced less than 10% of the people on the government payroll, but the damage was done. For many years after that, government jobs were given to party loyalists. The quality and honesty of government service suffered accordingly.

| Andrew Jackson

Eaton Scandal. Andrew Jackson's mediocre Cabinet was quickly bogged down in a scandal over the wife of Secretary of War John Eaton. Eaton had married the pretty daughter of a tavern keeper who had a very poor moral reputation. The wives of the other members of the administration refused to socialize with her. "Old Hickory" was very taken with Peggy Eaton and believed she was the victim of baseless gossip. He also remembered the gossip about his own beloved wife who had died shortly after he was elected, and he unwisely became a public champion for Mrs. Eaton. Jackson tried unsuccessfully to force Washington society to accept Peggy Eaton. Led by the well-born wife of Vice President John Calhoun, the ladies refused. Even Jackson's niece, who was his official hostess, left rather than entertain Mrs. Eaton in the White House.

The cabinet's limited ability suffered in the discord. Jackson eventually began seeking advice on policy from an informal group of advisors and friends, called the "kitchen cabinet" by his opponents. Secretary of State Martin Van Buren took advantage of the situation to ingratiate himself with the president. As a widower, Van Buren socialized freely with Mrs. Eaton and won the president's favor by doing so. As the discord in the cabinet grew worse, Van Buren resigned, knowing that would pressure the other secretaries to do the same. They did so, relieving Jackson of a difficult situation by removing the Eatons from the Washington elite. Van Buren was rewarded with the vice presidency during Jackson's second term.

Webster-Hayne Debate. The long-standing debate over the power of the states versus the power of the federal government was a key part of the conflict of the early 1800s. Early in 1830 the question was raised in the Senate and resulted in a spectacular debate between Robert Hayne of South Carolina and Daniel Webster of Massachusetts. The Webster-Hayne Debate was a memorable part of the long North-South conflict that preceded the Civil War.

The debate began over the unlikely topic of a resolution by the New England states to restrict the sale of land in the West. Hayne used the occasion to attack the northeast and the Tariff of Abominations. He publicly argued in favor of the doctrine of nullification. This doctrine taught that any state could nullify a law of the United States that was contrary to the Constitution as they understood it. Nullification had been espoused by no lesser person than Vice President Calhoun in a 1828 document called the "South Carolina Exposition." Hayne saw it as a way to protect his region from domination by the rest of the Union.

The gallery of the Senate was full as people came to listen to Webster's reply. He used all of his great skill to speak in favor of the Union and federal power to force obedience from the states. He argued that if the states were free to go their own way at will, then the country was united only by a "rope of sand." He attacked nullification as a danger to the nation. Webster's arguments were summarized in his stirring statement, "Liberty and Union, now and forever, one and inseparable." Webster's speech was printed and widely read, making him a hero among those who favored a strong Union.

Split with Calhoun. No one was certain where Jackson stood on the issue of states' rights. He consistently opposed internal improvements within any one state and sought to keep federal taxes and expenses low—basic pro-state positions. He was also a slave-owning plantation farmer, but he had not made any clear statements one way or the other. The states' rights supporters, led by Calhoun, hoped to gain his public support for their favorite cause. They chose a party celebrating Thomas Jefferson's birthday as the ideal occasion. A whole series of toasts were offered celebrating the Jeffersonian ideals of the sovereignty of the states. Jackson, however, had been warned of what would happen and had carefully prepared his own toast. When his turn came he spoke the words, "Our Union: It must be preserved!" A shaken Calhoun tried to salvage the evening with the answer, "The Union, next to our liberty, most dear!" However, the damage was done. Jackson had declared himself as a Union man.

Vice President John Calhoun was hoping to be Andrew Jackson's successor. As a potential future president, Calhoun hid his personal views and publicly supported the Union. He had deliberately not attached his name to the "South Carolina Exposition" on nullification. However, his presidential hopes were dashed when he and Jackson split over the Peggy Eaton scandal as well as personal and policy differences. Calhoun retired from the vice presidency near the end of his term and returned to the Senate as the leader of those who espoused nullification and the power of the states.

The National Bank. Andrew Jackson had a passionate distrust of the National Bank, which he called the "moneyed monster." The director, Nicholas Biddle, did little to help the situation by his "loans" and payments to prominent congressmen, including Daniel Webster. Jackson believed the bank was a danger to the nation. He shared the Western distrust of powerful financial institutions that foreclosed on farm mortgages. He did not understand national finances or the way the bank helped the West by its sound money policy.

Henry Clay, who was likely to be the National Republican presidential candidate, saw the bank as a way to undermine Old Hickory's popularity. The bank was due to be rechartered in 1836. Clay forced a bill through Congress rechartering the National Bank in 1832, a presidential election year. He assumed Jackson would have to sign it and alienate his Western followers or veto it and alienate the businessmen of the nation.

Jackson did veto the bill, sending a scathing message back to Congress. Jackson attacked the bank in violent, colorful terms that set the issue as a war between the rich and the poor. His arguments had little substance but a great deal of popular appeal among the financially ignorant public who loved him. Clay foolishly believed the message would harm Jackson because of its angry tone and lack of intelligent argument.

A Growing Nation (1820–1855) | Unit 5

Election of 1832. The election of 1832 was the first in which the candidates were chosen by national political conventions. Jackson on the Democratic ticket squared off against Henry Clay who had received the National Republican nomination. The National Bank was the central issue of the campaign. Clay had copies of Jackson's veto printed up to use against him. The veto message, however, was accepted as truth by the general public and cemented Jackson's image as a defender of the common man. Wealthier people who had reason to be concerned by the attack did not vote for him anyway. Jackson won the election easily.

Match these items (answers may be used more than once).

1.40 _____ party loyalists get government jobs
1.41 _____ King Mob
1.42 _____ "Liberty and Union, now and forever, one and inseparable."
1.43 _____ Nicholas Biddle
1.44 _____ Van Buren used it to gain Jackson's favor
1.45 _____ issue in 1832 election
1.46 _____ rotation in office
1.47 _____ Calhoun tried to get a states' rights position by Jackson
1.48 _____ "Our Union: It must be preserved!"
1.49 _____ senator publicly supported nullification
1.50 _____ hurt the honesty and quality of government service
1.51 _____ Jackson's "moneyed monster"
1.52 _____ Jackson insisted on publicly supporting a woman against moral rumors
1.53 _____ caused the resignation of the entire cabinet
1.54 _____ Jackson had to flee the building to avoid injury
1.55 _____ Jackson vetoed it in 1832
1.56 _____ nullification would mean Union joined by a "rope of sand"
1.57 _____ Congress passed bill to recharter it in 1832

a. Spoils system
b. Jackson inauguration
c. Webster-Hayne Debate
d. National Bank
e. Eaton Scandal
f. Jefferson birthday dinner

Answer these questions.

1.58 What injury gave Jackson a personal hatred for the British?
_____
_____

1.59 How did Jackson get the bullets that stayed in his body?
_____

1.60 What were three Western prejudices Jackson took to the White House?

a. _____

b. _____

c. _____

1.61 What is the doctrine of nullification?
_____
_____

1.62 What was the name of Jackson's group of informal advisors?
_____

1.63 Who was Jackson's first vice president?
_____

1.64 Who was vice president during Jackson's second term?
_____

1.65 Why did Henry Clay force a rechartering of the National Bank?
_____
_____
_____
_____

A Growing Nation (1820–1855) | Unit 5

The End of the Jacksonian Era

Nullification Crisis. The Tariff of Abominations was a major issue in South Carolina. Congress voted in 1832 to reduce the tariff to more moderate levels, but it did not satisfy the Carolina "nullies." That same year they gained control of the state legislature and declared the tariff null and void in South Carolina. They also threatened to leave the Union if the federal government tried to enforce it.

Andrew Jackson was not about to take such a threat calmly. He sent reinforcements and supplies to federal forts in South Carolina. He also quietly prepared a larger army for use, if needed. He then denounced nullification and privately threatened to hang its supporters. The Southern leaders, especially Calhoun, knew Jackson well enough to take his threats seriously.

Jackson requested the passage of the Force Bill in early 1833 to grant authorization for troops to collect the tariffs in South Carolina. Calhoun led the assault on the bill. He had a great deal of support because of the rise of sectionalism in the nation. The nationalism of the post-War of 1812 era had given way to local loyalties to states and regions. Calhoun and Webster traded brilliant oratory in the Senate trying to force their views. Henry Clay finally brokered a compromise. A new tariff was passed that would gradually reduce the tax over the next ten years. Calhoun, realizing that he was on the verge of civil war, accepted the compromise and convinced his state to drop the nullification. South Carolina agreed but added the empty gesture of nullifying the Force Bill which had been signed into law.

Trail of Tears. The issue of what to do with the Native Americans who still owned large stretches of land east of the Mississippi had been left unanswered for years. Jackson was not a man to avoid an issue. In 1830 he proposed moving the tribes to new land west of the Mississippi where they would be "forever" free of encroachment by white settlers. Jackson deluded himself into believing this was a benevolent policy that was in the best interest of the Native Americans.

Many members of Congress opposed the Removal Act, particularly those who were strong Christians or who came from districts

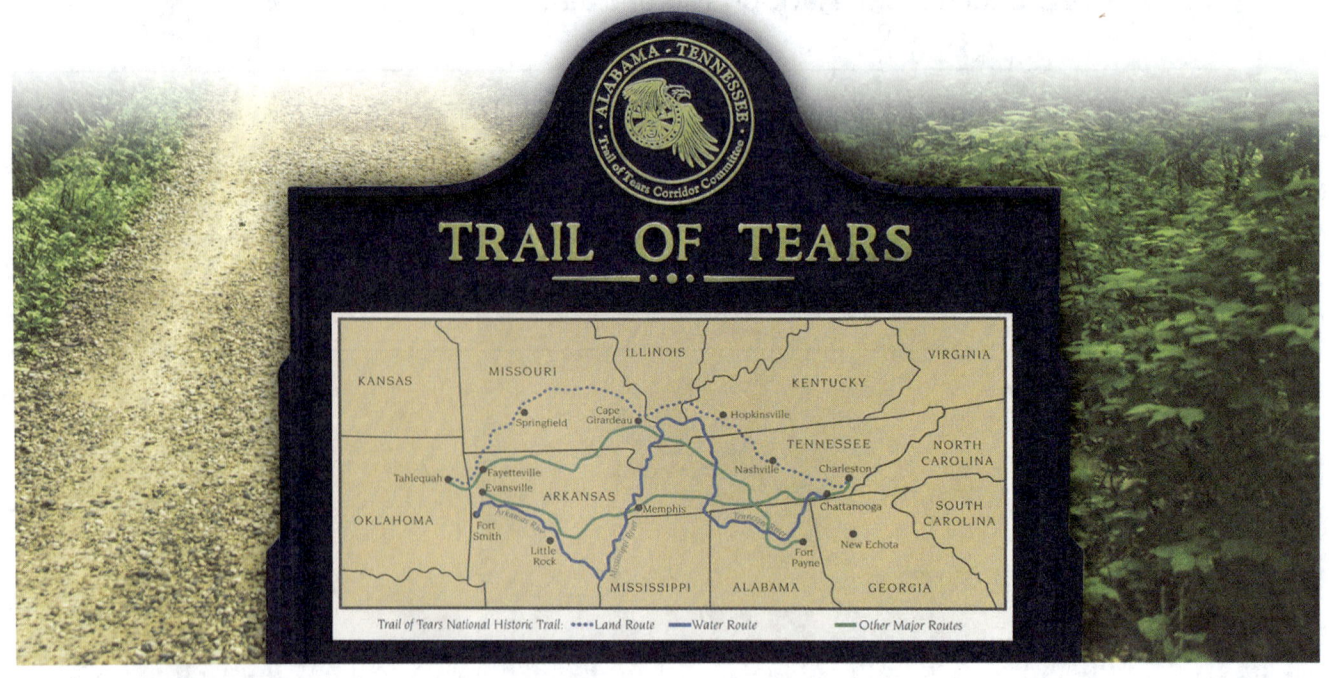

| National Historic Trail

with strong Christian constituents. However, Jackson put the full force of his persuasive and political powers behind the act. It was passed in 1830, granting the Native Americans land in the West and the money to move them.

Jackson moved enthusiastically to carry out his program. Many of the tribes accepted the inevitable and signed treaties giving up their land. They moved west suffering from hunger, disease, and exposure on the way. Georgia, Mississippi, and Alabama made it clear they would seize the Native American land whether treaties were signed or not. Jackson did nothing to discourage them.

The Cherokee People of Georgia, who had largely taken up American life, fought back. They refused to sign a new treaty and challenged Georgia in court when the state annexed their land. The Cherokee won. The Supreme Court said the state of Georgia had no authority over the federal treaties that gave the Native Americans their land, but it was no use. Andrew Jackson would not give the Supreme Court the backing it needed to protect the Native Americans. Jackson is reported to have said, "John Marshall has made his decision; now let him enforce it."

The Cherokee were finally removed by the army in 1838. They were crowded into prison camps and then forced to make the long journey west. About four thousand Cherokee died on the way. They called it "the Trail of Tears."

Some of the Native American People chose to go to war rather than leave. The Sauk People in the Northwest Territory fought under the leadership of their chief, Black Hawk. The Black Hawk War quickly ended in a victory by the American army. The Sauks were removed to Iowa. The Seminoles took advantage of the wild terrain of Florida to hold out until 1842. The Seminole War was the longest and most expensive war with a Native American people in American history. They were finally defeated and moved west also.

The Native American removal was one of the blackest marks on an already poor American record. Thousands of Native Americans died after being forced to surrender their land to the greed of white settlers. Even then, the promise that their new land would not be taken was never kept. Within a generation, they were facing the same pressure to give up their land to new settlers who had crossed the Mississippi. The whole thing was all the more tragic because of how many people believed it was good for the Native Americans. Sinful human beings have an incredible ability to justify their own wrongdoing.

National Bank. Jackson saw the election of 1832 as a mandate from the people in his battle with the National Bank. Therefore, he decided to kill the bank instead of just letting it run until its charter ended in 1836. He first had to fire his secretary of the treasury and appoint a new one that would go along with his plan. That accomplished, he began to remove federal money from the National Bank and put it into "pet banks" in various states. The banks were chosen in large part for their loyalty to Jackson, and some funds were wasted in the process. Henry Clay succeeded in convincing Congress to censure Jackson for this "unconstitutional" action. The rebuff had no effect on Jackson's actions.

Nicholas Biddle reacted in a way that confirmed Jackson's worst fears about the National Bank. He deliberately reduced credit to the point that businesses began to fail and the country fell on hard times. It was just this kind of power that Jackson did not want a private corporation to have! Jackson refused to budge even when hit with a long stream of petitions from struggling businessmen. He told them to take their petitions to Biddle. In the end, public pressure forced Biddle to surrender, relax credit, and close the bank.

The return to good times brought about a spiral of inflation and land speculation. Many of the western banks began issuing money with no reliable value. Jackson inadvertently encouraged the national self-confidence that fueled the speculation. In 1835, he became the only U.S. president ever to pay off the entire national debt! Fearful of the effects of wild speculation, Jackson issued the *Specie Circular*, a decree that all land purchased from the federal government had to be paid for in *specie*: gold or silver coins. That set the scene for the Panic of 1837.

Analysis. Andrew Jackson was a highly successful president. He did just about everything he wanted to do in office even if it was not good for the nation. He considered the president to be the representative of the people and acted independently of the other branches of government. He vetoed more laws than any president before him. He used his popularity to push through laws he wanted and to destroy the National Bank. His forceful foreign policy reopened American trade with the British West Indies and gained payments from Europe for American ships seized during the Napoleonic Wars. His actions as president increased the power and prestige of the office. His strong response to the Nullification Crisis undoubtedly saved the Union. He was so popular when he left office that he was even able to handpick his own successor whose term is considered a part of the Jacksonian Era.

Election of 1836. Jackson decided not to run again and made sure that Martin Van Buren received the Democratic nomination for president in 1836. The National Republicans had adopted the name of Whig by then and ran several candidates. Van Buren defeated the Whigs, led by William Henry Harrison, using Jackson's popularity. However, Van Buren inherited all the problems and enemies Jackson had created during his eight years in office. He took them on without having either the general's popularity or his fiery will. It was a disastrous combination.

Martin Van Buren. Martin Van Buren (1782-1862) was the first American president born after the Declaration of Independence. He was born in New York where he practiced law as a young man. He served in the New York legislature and the Senate. He won the governorship of New York in 1828 but gave it up to serve as Jackson's secretary of state. Van Buren was a professional politician known as the "Little Magician" for his skill at manipulating events to his advantage. He won the election solely on the support of Andrew Jackson. He had deliberately built his friendship with Old Hickory for just such a purpose.

The Panic of 1837. Land speculation in the West had become a major American pastime. Thousands of people bought land hoping to hold it and sell it for a profit later. The purchases were often made with loans from unstable banks. People were making huge profits only as long as credit was available. The prosperity of the nation was on shifting ground, and it gave way in 1837 just after Van Buren took office.

Jackson's destruction of the National Bank had removed one of the major safeguards in the American banking system. His *Specie Circular* had caused a sudden demand for gold and silver that drained Eastern bank reserves. Crop failures and a financial panic in England hit at the same time. British banks called in (demanded payment for) their foreign loans. Banks in America closed, people lost their savings, businesses closed, land sales fell, tariff income fell as trade was reduced, and unemployment hit the masses of common people.

Van Buren's popularity, never very high, quickly plummeted. He could do little to help in the situation. He did get federal money moved to an independent treasury to protect it from being lost when pet banks collapsed. His popularity was also hurt by anti-slave forces who opposed the Seminole War (they did not want another slave state in Florida) and pro-slave forces who wanted him to annex Texas. His single term was largely unfruitful.

Complete these sentences.

1.66 _____ was the only president ever to pay off the entire national debt.

1.67 The Cherokee called their removal west the _____.

1.68 Jackson removed federal money from the National Bank and put it into so-called _____ banks.

1.69 In 1832 South Carolina voted to nullify the _____.

1.70 Jackson's financial policies led to the _____ that hurt Van Buren.

1.71 Henry Clay succeeded in convincing the Senate to _____ Jackson because of the removal of federal funds from the National Bank.

1.72 The Panic of 1837 was largely caused by _____ in land.

1.73 The _____ War was the longest and most expensive Indian war in American history.

1.74 The Supreme Court sided with the _____ Native Americans in their legal fight with the state of Georgia.

1.75 The _____ Bill authorized troops to enforce the tariff in South Carolina.

1.76 Jackson privately threatened to _____ the nullifiers.

1.77 The Sauk People fought the _____ War to avoid removal from their land.

1.78 Andrew Jackson's hand-picked successor was _____.

1.79 The Southern states annexed Native American land in defiance of the Supreme Court because _____ would not support the Native Americans.

1.80 "Little Magician" was the nickname of _____.

A Growing Nation (1820–1855) | Unit 5

Answer these questions.

1.81 What was the compromise that ended the Nullification Crisis?
_____
_____
_____

1.82 What did Jackson think he would accomplish with the Removal Act?
_____
_____

1.83 How did Jackson kill the National Bank?
_____
_____

Review the material in this section in preparation for the Self Test. The Self Test will check your mastery of this particular section. The items missed on this Self Test will indicate specific areas where restudy is needed for mastery.

SELF TEST 1

Match these people (each answer, 2 points).

1.01 _____ inventor of the cotton gin
1.02 _____ leader of nullification and states' rights
1.03 _____ "Old Hickory"
1.04 _____ his wife's social problems caused Jackson's entire cabinet to resign
1.05 _____ won the presidency in 1824 in the House of Representatives with a "corrupt bargain"
1.06 _____ president of the Bank of the U.S.
1.07 _____ the Little Magician
1.08 _____ Massachusetts representative, defender of the Union
1.09 _____ the Great Compromiser
1.010 _____ pro-nullification senator who had a famous debate with Webster

a. Henry Clay
b. Andrew Jackson
c. Daniel Webster
d. John Calhoun
e. Martin Van Buren
f. John Quincy Adams
g. John Eaton
h. Robert Hayne
i. Nicholas Biddle
j. Eli Whitney

Name the item or person described (each answer, 4 points).

1.011 _____ tax passed in 1828 to embarrass Adams by how high it was; it passed anyway, to the anger of the old South

1.012 _____ no slavery in the Louisiana Territory north of 36° 30′, Maine admitted as a free state, Missouri as a slave state

1.013 _____ machine that led to the South becoming dependent on cotton and slavery

1.014 _____ political party created by Andrew Jackson

1.015 _____ political party led by Henry Clay after the split of the Democratic-Republicans

1.016 _____ "Old Man Eloquent," successfully opposed the Gag Rule in Congress, collapsed and died in the House of Representatives

1.017 _____ depression caused by land speculation and Jackson's financial policies that hurt Van Buren's presidency

A Growing Nation (1820–1855) | Unit 5

1.018 _____ government jobs were given to loyal supporters of the newly-elected leaders

1.019 _____ the name the Cherokee used to described their forced trip west of the Mississippi, away from their land

1.020 _____ presidential decree by Andrew Jackson that all payments for land must be made in gold or silver

Complete the following (each answer, 5 points).

1.021 What was the Doctrine of Nullification?
_____
_____
_____

1.022 Why was the presidency of John Quincy Adams so unsuccessful?
_____
_____
_____
_____

1.023 Briefly describe Andrew Jackson's personal history before he was president.
_____
_____
_____
_____

1.024 What did Jackson do to face the Nullification Crisis and how was it resolved?
_____
_____
_____

1.025 Why did Henry Clay try to recharter the National Bank early and what was the effect?
_____
_____
_____

Unit 5 | **A Growing Nation (1820–1855)**

1.026 Describe Andrew Jackson's first inaugural reception at the White House.

_____
_____
_____

Answer true or false (each answer, 1 point).

1.027 _____ Jackson's group of informal advisors were called the "parlor cabinet."

1.028 _____ Henry Clay was never elected president.

1.029 _____ Jackson's campaign slogan in 1828, when he first won the presidency, was "Jackson and Reform."

1.030 _____ John Calhoun began his political career as a strong nationalist.

1.031 _____ The slavery issue was avoided in the early 1800s, but the North and South opposed each other over the tariff instead.

1.032 _____ John Calhoun was the spokesman for the western part of the nation.

1.033 _____ The South was very independent, producing its own food, cash crops, and manufactured goods.

1.034 _____ Before the time of Andrew Jackson presidential candidates were chosen by national convention of political parties.

1.035 _____ Andrew Jackson hand-picked Daniel Webster as his successor.

1.036 _____ The Seminole War was one of the shortest Indian wars in American history.

80/100 SCORE _____ TEACHER _____ _____
                                    initials   date

2. MANIFEST DESTINY

In 1845 a newspaper article in the *Democratic Review* spoke of America's "manifest destiny" to move across the continent to claim the land given by God for her fast-growing population. The term quickly became popular. It became the historical title for the great American drive to gain land from sea to sea.

America had always been a land with a frontier. The frontier moved as older sections filled up with people and became more "civilized." The American urge to move west was almost an addiction. Thousands did it, hoping for a better life. They faced intense hardships and death, but these hardy people built the wild lands of the West into the cities, farms, and industries we know today.

This section will cover the last major phase of manifest destiny from 1840 to 1853, the expansion to the Pacific Ocean. Differences with Great Britain were settled on the borders of Maine and the Oregon Territory. Texas became independent from Mexico and joined the Union. A war with Mexico brought in the American southwest and California. Finally, in 1853 a piece of land, called the Gadsden Purchase, was bought from Mexico to allow a coast-to-coast railroad. Thus, manifest destiny was fulfilled, and America had all of the land that would become the forty-eight contiguous states.

SECTION OBJECTIVES

Review these objectives. When you have completed this section, you should be able to:

1. Name the leaders of the era and explain their accomplishments.
2. Describe the presidency of Andrew Jackson and its effect on America.
3. Trace the development of the slavery and tariff issues from 1820 to 1855.
4. Define Manifest Destiny and describe its course in America.
5. Describe the course of the Texas Revolution and Mexican War.
9. Describe the compromises that kept the nation together and what ended them.
10. Describe the changes in America and American life in this era.

VOCABULARY

Study these words to enhance your learning success in this section.

artillery (är til′ u rē). A branch of the army armed with large-caliber, crew-served mounted firearms.

asylum (a sī′ lum). Protection from arrest and extradition given to political or other refugees by a nation.

continental divide (kon′ ti nen′ tl de vīd). A ridge of land separating streams that flow to opposite sides of a continent.

protégé (prōt′ e zhā). A person under the care and protection of an influential person, usually for the furthering of his career.

siesta (sē es′ ta). An afternoon nap or rest.

Unit 5 | **A Growing Nation (1820–1855)**

The Northern Border

Log Cabin Campaign. The election of 1840 gave the Whigs a chance at the presidency. Martin Van Buren ran for re-election on the Democratic ticket in spite of his fall in popularity. The Whigs chose William Henry Harrison with running mate John Tyler. Henry Clay wanted the nomination, but Clay's political opinions were too well-known. The Whigs wanted a noncontroversial candidate. They chose Harrison because he was a popular general who won victories against the Native Americans at Tippecanoe and the British at the Thames. Moreover, his views on the issues of the day were unknown. In fact, he deliberately avoided taking any positions on such things as tariffs, the National Bank and internal improvements.

The real focus of the campaign was created when a Democratic newspaper gave the Whigs a slogan. The paper derided Harrison as a man who would be content with "a pension, a log cabin, and a barrel of hard cider." The Whigs jumped at the accusation calling Harrison the "Log Cabin and Hard Cider" candidate, a poor, hard-working common man. (Harrison was actually a wealthy land owner.) All over the country rallies were held with log cabins mounted on wagons and barrels of hard cider. The catchy phrase "Tippecanoe and Tyler, too" added to the circus atmosphere of the campaign. Harrison won by a large electoral but small popular margin.

William Henry Harrison. William Henry Harrison (1773-1841) was sixty-eight years old at the time of his election. He had been born in Virginia on his family's plantation. His father had signed the Declaration of Independence and served in the Continental Congress. Harrison joined the army as a young man and served until 1798. He later served as an official in the Northwest Territory and was one of that region's first representatives to Congress. He served for twelve years as the governor of the Indiana Territory. It was as the head of that

| Log Cabin and Hard Cider

territory's militia that he won the battle of Tippecanoe in 1811. He was a general in the War of 1812 and won the Battle of the Thames in Ontario. After that, he served in the House and the Senate. He ran for President as a Whig in 1836 and lost before winning in 1840.

Harrison had the shortest administration of any president in American history. He gave a very long inaugural address in cold, rainy weather and caught a cold. Less than a month later, the cold developed into pneumonia. On April 4, 1841, 31 days after his inauguration, Harrison died. (Presidential inaugurations took place in March until the 20th Amendment to the Constitution in 1933 changed it to January.)

Tyler, Too. John Tyler (1790-1862) was the first man to move from the vice presidency to the presidency because the latter died in office. He had, like Harrison, been born into an established Virginia family. He took up the practice of law with his father as a young man. He served in the House, the Senate, and as governor of Virginia before becoming vice president.

Tyler was a Democrat in Whig clothing. He had been put on the ticket as a supporter of states' rights to draw the Southern vote. His

Section 2 | 29

succession to the presidency doomed the Whig agenda. He proceeded to veto a new National Bank, higher tariffs, and internal improvements passed by the nationalistic Whig Congress. He quickly lost all of his Whig support in the government. His entire cabinet, except Secretary of State Daniel Webster, resigned. His enemies took to calling Tyler "His Accidency."

Maine's Boundary. Daniel Webster did not resign because he was in the middle of negotiations with Great Britain. Relations with the former mother country had reached one of their periodic boiling points. In 1837 a small, short-lived rebellion in Canada had been aided by many northern Americans before it was put down. An American vessel supplying the rebels with arms was attacked and destroyed by British troops on the American side of the Niagara River. In 1840 a Canadian citizen who claimed to have been a part of the raid was arrested for murder. The British government threatened war if the man was executed. (He was later acquitted.) The tension grew in 1841 when the British officials in the Bahamas gave asylum to a group of Virginia slaves who had rebelled and captured an American ship.

The two sides finally came to the negotiating table over the boundary of Maine. Both claimed parts of the land along the border. The treaty of 1783, which ended the Revolution, was not very clear on the matter. In the early 1840s, lumberjacks from Canada and the U.S. were fighting over the right to harvest trees in the disputed area. The fighting expanded and the militia was called in. The so-called "Aroostook War" threatened to become a real one. The two sides met and finally set an agreeable border. The Webster-Ashburton Treaty of 1842 gave the Americans more of the land but gave the British access to a route they needed for a military road. It also settled all of the other outstanding differences between the countries, except for the question of Oregon.

Congress was furious at the treaty. They were in no mood to give up land that they thought

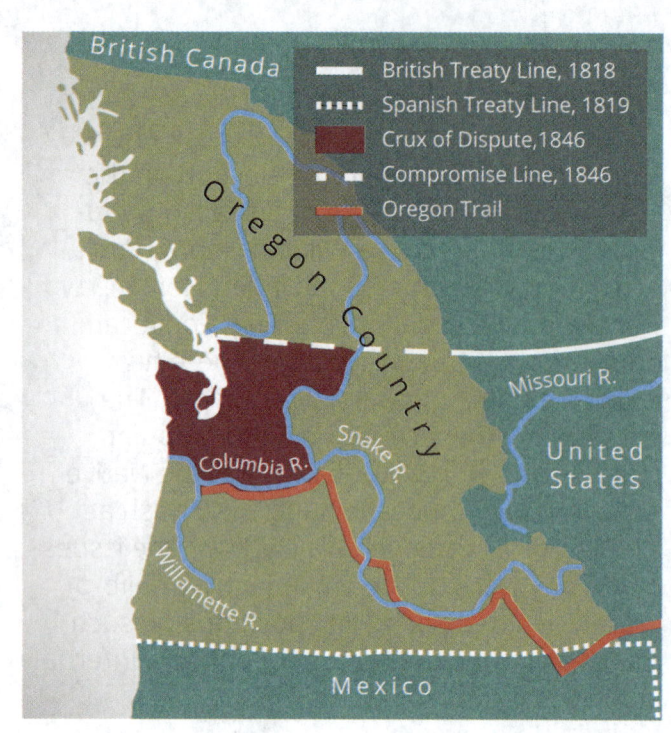

| Oregon Territory

was rightfully American. Webster, however, showed them an ancient map that implied that the British had rightful claim to the entire area in dispute! The treaty easily passed the Senate after that. Ironically, the British accepted the treaty because they had an ancient map that showed the Americans had rightful claim to the whole area!

Oregon Territory. Both Britain and America had claims to the beautiful and fertile Oregon Territory. At that time, Oregon included all of the land between California and the southern tip of Alaska west of the continental divide. Spain had given up her claim to the area in the Adams-Onis Treaty which had given Florida to the United States and set the borders of the Louisiana Territory. A Russian claim south of latitude 54° 40' was extinguished by treaty in the 1820s. Unable to settle their own differences there, Britain and the U.S. had agreed to occupy the land jointly in 1818. That agreement was renewed in 1827, since neither side would compromise.

Unit 5 | **A Growing Nation (1820–1855)**

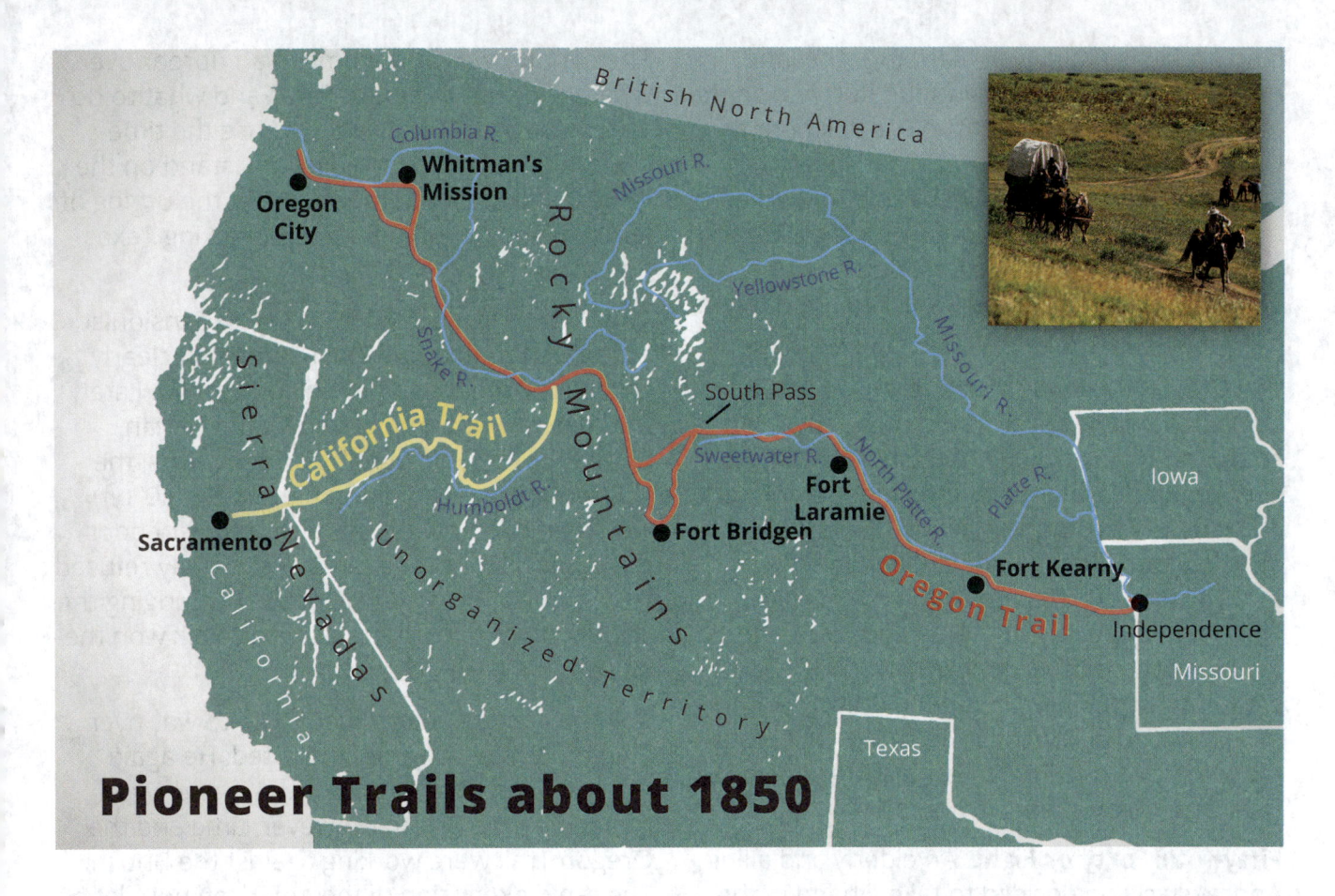

Pioneer Trails about 1850

The crux of the debate was a section of land north of the Columbia River up to the 49th parallel, the border between Canada and the U.S. on the east side of the Rocky Mountains. America wanted this land because it included Puget Sound, the only good harbor along the entire section of seacoast. The British were willing to concede the land south of the Columbia, but steadfastly refused to extend the previously established 49th parallel border requested by the Americans. The Americans on the other hand, did not want a section of land on the Pacific coast without access to a harbor. Matters stood this way for years.

Oregon Trail. The Rocky Mountains had been explored by mountain men who lived in the wild, trapping fur animals. Their knowledge provided the information Americans needed to reach their most western lands. One of these men named Jedidiah Smith discovered South Pass, a route over the Rockies that could be traversed by a wagon. That pass was surveyed in 1842 by John Frémont, an American army officer. Slowly, the information needed to bring people and their wagons safely into Oregon was accumulated.

The British had established the first permanent settlements in Oregon. These were fur-trading posts organized by the Hudson Bay Company around 1825 under the leadership of John McLoughlin, known as "the Father of Oregon." The first permanent American settlement was a group of missionaries who settled in the Willamette Valley in 1834. In 1836 Presbyterian missionary Marcus Whitman brought his wife over the long, dangerous route to live in Oregon. She was the first of a flood of women and children who came with their men to make Oregon their home.

Americans became enraptured with reports coming out of Oregon. The missionaries, trappers, and explorers sent glowing reports of the

Section 2 | 31

A Growing Nation (1820–1855) | Unit 5

land and its suitability for farming. The land between the Mississippi and the Rockies, on the other hand, was labeled "The Great American Desert" by an army explorer. That vast grassland was believed to be unsuitable for settled farming. It was primarily an obstacle to Oregon and California-bound settlers. Beginning in 1843, thousands of pioneers risked the dangers of the desert to reach the riches of Oregon.

The Oregon Trail was the route these brave souls traveled. It began in Independence, Missouri and covered 2,000 of the hardest miles ever regularly traveled by families and animals. The trip took six months. Native Americans attacked and rivers flooded. People ran out of food. Wagons broke and draft animals died. Hundreds of people also died and were buried along the route in lonely graves with bare wood markers. There had been only a handful of Americans in Oregon in 1840. By 1850, there were over 12,000. The Americans were going to take Oregon by sheer numbers.

Fifty-four Forty or Fight. An elderly and ailing Andrew Jackson decided to take a hand in the election of 1844. He hand picked the Democratic candidate James K. Polk, a strong expansionist, and campaigned for him by letters from his sickbed. He also persuaded Tyler not to run because he would take votes from Polk. The Whigs nominated the venerable Henry Clay.

The country was at the time in an uproar over whether or not to annex Texas and what to do about Oregon. Clay decided to use the time-honored method of avoiding any stand on the issues. Polk, on the other hand, at the urging of Jackson, spoke out in favor of annexing Texas and acquiring all of Oregon.

The Democrats cashed in on the expansionist attitude of the nation. Their campaign clearly called for America to have all of Oregon. Later, that desire was summarized by the slogan, "Fifty-four Forty or Fight!" In other words, the U.S. would get all of Oregon up to 54° 40' or would go to war with Britain. It was very poor diplomacy but great politics. Henry Clay refused to commit one way or the other, misjudging the popularity of the issues yet again. Polk won the election on a very close vote.

Polk was not as determined to go to war over Oregon as his campaign indicated. He again offered to set the boundary at 49° and was refused by the British. However, time and the Oregon Trail were working against the British. The rapid expansion of the American population in the territory endangered the British claims. The Americans could just take all of the land that they wanted, and the tiny British population could not oppose them. In 1846 the British themselves offered to extend the 49th parallel border, and the Americans quickly agreed.

Match these people.

2.1 _____ Father of Oregon

2.2 _____ discovered South Pass

2.3 _____ Whig candidate in 1844

2.4 _____ Democratic candidate in 1844

2.5 _____ president with the shortest administration

2.6 _____ first vice president to become president because of a death

a. William H. Harrison
b. John Tyler
c. James K. Polk
d. Henry Clay
e. Daniel Webster
f. Jedidiah Smith
g. John McLoughlin

Complete these sentences.

2.7 William Henry Harrison's 1840 campaign called him the _____ and _____ candidate.

2.8 _____ did not get the Whig nomination in 1840 because he had publicly expressed his opinions on the issues.

2.9 Tyler was a Whig president, but he held _____ ideas on the issues.

2.10 The boundary of Maine was settled by the _____ Treaty.

2.11 Thousands of Americans reached Oregon by traveling the _____ from Independence, Missouri.

2.12 Britain and America disputed the Oregon land north of the _____ and south of the _____ .

2.13 America wanted the disputed Oregon land because it wanted a _____ on the Pacific coast.

2.14 The slogan for those who wanted all of the Oregon Territory was _____ .

2.15 The catchy, rhyming phase used by Harrison's campaign in 1840 was _____ .

2.16 President John Tyler's enemies called him "_____."

2.17 The battle that broke out between lumberjacks in Maine over disputed land was called the _____ War.

2.18 The Great Plains were called the Great _____ in the 1840s.

2.19 The border of Oregon was set at the _____ parallel.

2.20 Tyler vetoed _____ , _____ , and _____ .

2.21 Polk won the 1844 election because he publicly favored annexing _____ and acquiring all of _____ .

2.22 _____ was a missionary who brought his wife to Oregon in 1836.

2.23 Congress accepted the Webster-Ashburton Treaty because Webster found a map that showed that _____ had claim to the entire area in dispute.

2.24 The Oregon Trail was about _____ miles long.

Section 2 | 33

Texas and Polk

Americans in Texas. America's claims to Texas were surrendered in 1819 by the Adams-Onis Treaty with Spain; however, land-hungry Americans wanted to farm the rich lands of east Texas that faced them across the border. Spain agreed to allow some to enter under special conditions. Moses Austin negotiated one such agreement with Spain in 1820. Austin was given a large tract of land along the Brazos River and given permission to settle three hundred families there. The settlers had to become Catholics, be of good character, and swear allegiance to the king of Spain. The Spanish government hoped to gain a tax-paying population for their vast domain and defenses against the Native American Peoples of the region.

Moses Austin died before he could execute his agreement. His son, Stephen Austin, settled the "First Three Hundred" in Texas beginning in 1821. In that same year, Mexico won its independence from Spain. Austin made the difficult journey to Mexico City to have his agreement confirmed by the new government. It was, and many others were granted in the years that followed. One important late settler was Sam Houston, a former Tennessee governor and friend of Andrew Jackson.

By 1835 about 30,000 Americans were living in Texas. Most were law-abiding settlers but some were men avoiding the law in America. "G.T.T." (Gone to Texas) was a note that was often left behind when a man found it necessary to get out from under the jurisdiction of the United States.

In spite of the requirement that they swear allegiance to the Mexican government, most of the settlers continued to think of themselves as Americans. They often defied the requirement of becoming Catholic and brought enslaved people into Texas in violation of the law. The independent settlers clashed with corrupt local officials and soldiers who were often little more than uniformed bandits. The Americans also were disturbed by the continuous instability of the Mexican government.

A revolt broke out in Texas in 1832 over a decree that forbade any more Americans to settle in the land. A revolt was also going on in Mexico City. The new president, General Antonio Lopez de Santa Anna, accepted the changes in Texas. Stephen Austin went to Mexico City in 1833 to petition that Texas become a separate state in the Mexican federation and allow American immigration. He was arrested and spent almost a year in jail before he was released.

The Texas Revolution. The last straw came in 1835. Santa Anna suspended the constitution and declared himself dictator. Several of the Mexican states, including Texas, rose in revolt. Fighting began in Texas in October when Santa Anna's soldiers tried to force the settlers to turn in their weapons. It began as a fight for their rights under the suspended Mexican Constitution.

Santa Anna sent his brother-in-law and an army to occupy San Antonio to control the situation. The Texians (as they called themselves) set up a temporary government and put Sam Houston in command of the army. A request was sent to the United States for volunteers. They poured in from all over the South. The Americans attacked San Antonio, capturing it in December of 1835. This alarmed Santa Anna. He assembled an army of about 8,000 and invaded Texas, arriving at San Antonio on February 23, 1836.

The troops that had been left to hold San Antonio had taken shelter in a mission/ fortress called the Alamo. Houston sent Colonel Jim Bowie with orders to blow up the Alamo and retreat. Bowie and the resident commander, William Travis, decided to ignore their orders and defend the fort. They had 183 men including a group of Tennessee volunteers led by the famous backwoodsman, Davy Crockett.

The Battle of the Alamo has become a vibrant part of American folklore, even though the defense of the mission was in violation of the orders of Sam Houston. The men who held the fort acted with the highest courage and forced Santa Anna to pay a horrendous price for his victory. They also delayed the advance of his army for two critical weeks which bought Houston time to organize.

The defenders of the Alamo refused to surrender, even when surrounded by an army perhaps 30 times their numbers. Santa Anna besieged the mission unsuccessfully from February 23 to March 6. The expert American marksmen held the walls against all attacks. Finally, on the 6th, the Mexicans stormed the walls, overwhelming them by sheer numbers. The Americans fought hand-to-hand as they ran out of ammunition. On the dictator's orders, all of the defenders were killed. Santa Anna lost over a thousand of his own men in the siege to the defenders' 183.

Remember the Alamo. The Texan leaders had been meeting to discuss their plans when the Alamo was under attack. They confirmed Houston as commander of the army and decided to declare Texas independent on March 2. News of the Alamo angered and aroused the Texans. Further fuel was added later in the month when Santa Anna ordered the cold-blooded murder of 400 men who had surrendered at Goliad. To cries of "Remember the Alamo! Remember Goliad!", the Texans rallied to defend themselves.

The wily Sam Houston led the Mexicans on a long, winding chase through the rough Texas countryside. The retreat was unpopular, but Houston managed to hold it together. Every day his army grew larger while Santa Anna's grew wearier and smaller. Finally, on April 21, the Texans attacked at San Jacinto during the Mexican **siesta**. Over a thousand Mexican soldiers were killed or wounded while the Americans lost less than forty. Santa Anna was captured and signed a treaty giving Texas its independence.

Annexation Question. Andrew Jackson, who was president at the time, was in a quandary. Santa Anna repudiated the treaty he signed after San Jacinto as soon as he was safely back in Mexico. Extending official recognition to the Lone Star Republic (the flag of Texas had one star) might spark an unpopular war with Mexico. Jackson delayed until after the election of Van Buren and then recognized the Texas Republic just before he left office.

Texas wanted to be part of the United States and promptly applied for admission in 1837. A two-thirds majority was needed to approve the treaty of annexation and it failed. The reason was slavery. The northern states refused to admit such a large, slave-holding land. An attempt was made again in 1844, but it also failed for the same reason. However, popular opinion was building in favor of annexation.

In 1844 James K. Polk made Texas a major issue in his campaign. When Polk won the election, President John Tyler believed it was a mandate to add Texas to the Union. He arranged for Congress to annex the territory by a joint resolution requiring only a simple majority.

| Davy Crockett at the Alamo, preparing to die

Annexation passed in December of 1844 and Texas became a state one year later.

James K. Polk. James K. Polk (1795-1849) added more territory to the United States than any other president. Polk was born in North Carolina to Irish immigrants. His father speculated in land and became wealthy in America. The younger Polk graduated from the University of North Carolina and took up the practice of law in Tennessee. He became a close friend and **protégé** of Andrew Jackson earning the name "Young Hickory" because of the General's support. He served seven terms in the House of Representatives and was Speaker of the House under Jackson's presidency. He also was elected to one term as governor of Tennessee. The Democratic Party could not agree on Van Buren or his chief rival, Lewis Cass, for their candidate in 1844. With Jackson's backing, Polk was offered as a compromise candidate. He was the first "dark horse" candidate, a virtual unknown chosen when better-known candidates were not acceptable for some reason.

Polk was a highly successful president. He set four goals to accomplish while in office. He achieved all of them. The first two were to lower the tariff and establish an independent treasury. The latter was needed because the Whigs had repealed Van Buren's treasury plans and were unable to re-establish a national bank. The Walker Tariff (named after Secretary of the Treasury Robert Walker) passed in 1846. It lowered most of the tariffs and eliminated some altogether. The independent treasury was set up that same year and handled America's government funds until the Federal Reserve was set up in 1913.

Polk's third goal was to settle the Oregon boundary dispute, which was accomplished in 1846. Polk's last goal was to add California to the United States. This proved to be the most difficult and costly of his goals.

In 1844 California was owned by Mexico. It was sparsely populated with a few thousand

| Disputed Texas

Mexicans and even fewer foreigners, mostly Americans. Manifest Destiny Americans wanted the fertile lands of its coastal valleys and the fine harbor at San Francisco. Mexico, still smarting from the annexation of Texas, had broken off diplomatic relations and refused all offers to buy California. Tensions were also high because Mexico had defaulted on payments of claims it owed U.S. citizens. In 1845 Mexico refused to even receive the new American minister. Polk decided to get what he wanted by war.

Events in Texas. The treaty signed by Santa Anna had set the southern border of Texas at the Rio Grande River. Mexico claimed that the real border was the Nueces River further to the north. While he had been trying to negotiate for California, Polk had kept U.S. troops out of the disputed area. In January 1846 he ordered General Zachary Taylor to take up a position on the Rio Grande River. As he hoped, the Mexicans attacked Taylor on April 25, 1846, killing or wounding sixteen men. Polk sent a message to Congress asking for a declaration of war because of the shedding of "American blood on American soil" by the Mexicans. Congress passed the war resolution by a wide margin.

Unit 5 | **A Growing Nation (1820–1855)**

Answer true or false.

If the statement is false, change some nouns or adjectives to make it true.

2.25 _____ Moses Austin settled the "First Three Hundred" families on the Brazos River in Texas.

2.26 _____ Most of the defenders of the Alamo were killed.

2.27 _____ The annexation of Texas stalled over the issue of slavery.

2.28 _____ Texans won their independence at the Battle of Goliad.

2.29 _____ Andrew Jackson recognized the Lone Star Republic just before he left office.

2.30 _____ James K. Polk was called "Young Hickory."

2.31 _____ America had surrendered its claims to Texas in the Webster-Ashburton Treaty.

2.32 _____ Henry Clay was the first "dark horse" candidate for president.

2.33 _____ Polk was a successful president.

2.34 _____ Americans brought enslaved people into Texas in violation of Mexican law.

Answer these questions.

2.35 What are the names of three of the men who died at the Alamo?

a. _____ b. _____

c. _____

2.36 What were James K. Polk's four goals for his presidency?

a. _____ b. _____

c. _____ d. _____

2.37 What did G.T.T. mean?

_____

2.38 How did Polk provoke a war with Mexico?

_____

_____

2.39 What event in Mexico triggered the Texas Revolution?

_____

_____

Section 2 | 37

A Growing Nation (1820–1855) | Unit 5

2.40 What were the two rally cries of the Texas Revolution?

_____

_____

2.41 What was Sam Houston's strategy after the Alamo?

_____

_____

The Mexican War

Politics of War. Mexican-American relations had been bad for some time. Revolution after revolution had rocked the Mexican Republic since its creation in 1821. During these upheavals, Americans were killed, their property taken, treaties were ignored, and damages were promised but not paid. The proud Mexicans had also said that the annexation of Texas would be a declaration of war. However, the main reason that the war began in 1846 was Polk's desire for California. There was a serious concern that Mexico could not hold California, and it might wind up in hostile British hands. Polk wanted it safely in American hands along with the New Mexico territory to complete America's sea-to-sea Manifest Destiny.

The war was controversial in its own time. Many people questioned whether or not America had really been the innocent victim of a Mexican attack, as Polk declared. Illinois representative Abraham Lincoln tried to force the president to admit that Mexicans attacked Americans on Mexican soil. Abolitionists feared the war was a conspiracy to add slave territory to the nation. John Calhoun opposed the declaration of war, fearing the new land would divide the nation. Webster and Clay opposed it as a creation of the Democratic president. (Both of them lost sons in the battles that followed.)

The controversy did not keep the war from being generally popular, however, especially as American victories mounted. Thousands of volunteers poured into the army from all over the nation to supplement the professional army. The professional army was small, especially compared to the large army Mexico had amassed (needed because of the continuous upheaval there). However, the American army had a superior collection of junior officers who had been trained at the military academy at West Point. Many of the men who would lead the North and South in the coming years received their battle training in the Mexican War. Robert E. Lee, Ulysses S. Grant, Thomas J. (Stonewall) Jackson, George Meade, George McClellan, and George Pickett were a few of the many future Civil War leaders who served in Mexico. Thus, the war was one of the last united acts of the nation before the division over slavery became unavoidable.

New Mexico and California. The territory coveted by the United States quickly and easily came under American control. Neither New Mexico nor California had any substantial forces to oppose an American invasion. Under the command of Colonel Stephen Kearny, troops marched from Fort Leavenworth, Kansas to New Mexico in June of 1846. The more than

HISTORY & GEOGRAPHY 805

LIFEPAC TEST

NAME _____

DATE _____

SCORE _____

HISTORY & GEOGRAPHY 805: LIFEPAC TEST

Match the president with the events of his administration. Some answers will be used more than once (each answer, 2 points).

1. _____ shortest administration in history
2. _____ Mexican War
3. _____ Panic of 1837
4. _____ Tariff of Abominations
5. _____ "corrupt bargain"
6. _____ Nullification Crisis
7. _____ *Specie Circular*
8. _____ Compromise of 1850
9. _____ Kansas-Nebraska Act
10. _____ boundary of Maine settled
11. _____ boundary of Oregon settled
12. _____ died in office unable to resolve organization of the Mexican Cession
13. _____ National Bank closed
14. _____ Texas Revolution
15. _____ California's Bear Flag Republic

a. John Quincy Adams
b. Andrew Jackson
c. Martin Van Buren
d. William H. Harrison
e. John Tyler
f. James K. Polk
g. Zachary Taylor
h. Millard Fillmore
i. Franklin Pierce

Name the item described (each answer, 3 points).

16. _____ No slavery north of 36° 30' in the Louisiana Purchase, Maine admitted as a free state

17. _____ Fugitive Slave Act, California admitted as a free state

18. _____ Native Americans of the Southeast were forced to move to land beyond the Mississippi River

19. _____ America was destined to move across and occupy the entire continent

20. _____ Rally cry for Americans who wanted to claim all of the Oregon Territory

21. _____ Majestic, streamlined sailing ships that took over the high-speed ocean trade of the early to mid-1800s

22. _____ Most successful internal canal in American history

23. _____ Secondary issue fought over by the North and South after the slavery issue was avoided by the Missouri Compromise

24. _____ government jobs are given to the loyal followers of whoever won the election

25. _____ route taken by people from eastern America to reach Oregon over land

Match these people (each answer, 2 points).

26. _____ author of *Uncle Tom's Cabin*   a. Winfield Scott
27. _____ Mexican dictator, fought Americans   b. Henry Clay
           in Texas and in the Mexican War   c. John Calhoun
28. _____ conductor on Underground Railroad   d. Daniel Webster
29. _____ cotton gin, interchangeable parts   e. Harriet Beecher Stowe
30. _____ steel plow   f. Eli Whitney
31. _____ Great Compromiser   g. Sam Houston
32. _____ victor of Mexico City campaign   h. Stephen Douglas
33. _____ brought British textile machine   i. Samuel Morse
           information to America   j. Harriet Tubman
34. _____ sewing machine   k. Nicholas Biddle
35. _____ defender of the South, Doctrine of Nullification   l. Samuel Slater
36. _____ president of National Bank   m. John Deere
37. _____ victor in Texas Revolution   n. Elias Howe
38. _____ telegraph   o. Santa Anna
39. _____ great orator from the North, debated Hayne
           on the subject of states' rights and nullification
40. _____ pushed the Kansas-Nebraska Act through Congress

Answer true or false (each answer, 1 point).

41. _____ *Uncle Tom's Cabin* was very effective anti-slavery propaganda.

42. _____ Andrew Jackson made the American government more elitist and less responsible to the desires of the common man.

43. _____ The cotton gin made slavery very profitable and protected in the South.

44. _____ The Whig party favored states' rights, low taxes and slavery.

45. _____ Americans settled in Texas when it was still part of Mexico.

46. _____ The Mexican War was a training ground for the Civil War.

47. _____ Irish immigrants were usually poor and settled on farms in the Far West.

48. _____ John Tyler was the only president of this era to serve two terms.

49. _____ John Quincy Adams was more successful as a member of the House of Representatives than as president.

50. _____ Nullification was a doctrine that said any state could leave the Union if it did not like the way it was being run.

1,500 troops traveled down the Santa Fe Trail, a road set up by American merchants to trade with that isolated Mexican outpost. Kearny captured the city and the territory easily.

California was captured in a very colorful manner. John C. Frémont, an army topographer, had already explored much of the West, creating accurate maps and suggesting sites for forts. He appeared in California in 1845, supposedly on a scientific expedition, but probably under secret orders from President Polk to be ready to take it in the event of war. In any case, Frémont led a rebellion in June of 1846 that declared California an independent republic called the "Bear Flag Republic." By the time word reached Frémont of the war with Mexico, most of northern California was already in his hands. The rest followed shortly.

The situation was complicated when Commodore Robert Stockton sailed in with official orders to seize California. He took Santa Barbara and Los Angeles. He was joined by Kearny who had arrived overland from New Mexico with the same orders. The two commanders retook Los Angeles when it rebelled in September of 1846 and quarreled over who was in command. Frémont arrived and added his dubious authority to the fray. Kearny had Frémont arrested and sent back to Washington for a court martial. He was found guilty but was released by President Polk's orders. Thus, California was captured.

Northern Mexico Campaign. Zachary Taylor, whose troops had been attacked along the Rio Grande, did not wait for the official declaration from Washington. He knew he had a war with Mexico even though the politicians had not officially declared it. "Old Rough and Ready," as Taylor was known, was a popular commander. He was an easy-going man who dressed without regard for military protocol, often wearing a straw hat. He was a capable but not brilliant commander who was determined to press on with the job.

| Battle in Northern Mexico

In May, Taylor met the Mexican army at Palo Alto and Resaca de la Palma, both north of the Rio Grande. In both cases, the Americans won with far lighter casualties than the Mexicans. The skillful American **artillery** proved decisive in both victories. Taylor then went to the aid of Fort Texas which he had established near the mouth of the Rio Grande. He renamed it Fort Brown after the commander who had died defending it during the siege by the Mexican army. Acting without orders, Taylor then crossed the Rio Grande and captured the city of Matamoros without firing a shot.

The quick series of victories made Taylor a hero. The Whigs immediately began to talk of having him run for president in 1848, and Taylor did nothing to discourage the talk. Polk, a hard-core Jacksonian Democrat, was alarmed by the general's popularity. The president tried unsuccessfully to appoint a Democratic general to gain the laurels of victory, but Congress refused to cooperate.

In June Taylor was ordered south. He attacked the city of Monterrey in September of 1846. It was heavily fortified and American losses were heavy. The Americans eventually captured the town, using a technique borrowed from the Texans who took San Antonio during their revolution. The soldiers burrowed through the adobe walls of the city buildings, moving closer and closer to the city center, house by house. The Mexicans finally surrendered and received generous peace terms from the general. The terms were so generous that they were later repudiated by the U.S. government. Taylor was now ordered to hold what he had taken and send a large part of his army south to assist General Winfield Scott in a planned attack on the Mexican capital.

Taylor, however, believed his orders were intended to quiet him and cut off his political popularity. He ignored them and marched his reduced army south, reaching Buena Vista near the city of Saltillo in February of 1847. There he

| California's Bear Flag

was met by a huge army under the command of the revived Mexican dictator, Santa Anna.

Santa Anna had been in exile in Cuba when the war began. In exchange for a large bribe and passage into Mexico, he had offered to give America the land they wanted. Naively, James Polk believed him. Santa Anna returned to Mexico, took over the government and announced a great war to defend the nation against the barbarian invaders. He assembled an army of over 20,000 to meet Taylor who had about 6,500. He offered Taylor a chance to surrender in the face of the superior numbers. Taylor refused, even though he was outnumbered three to one.

The Battle of Buena Vista lasted two days. It was marked by the daring and skill of the junior officers who held out against the incredible odds. Taylor refused to retreat, even when some of his men recommended it. Again, the American artillery proved decisive, and it was the Mexicans who retreated. This remarkable victory confirmed Taylor's growing reputation as a national hero. He remained in northern Mexico for the rest of the war.

Doniphan. Kearny had divided his command at Santa Fe. A group of Missouri Mounted Volunteers were sent south under the command of Colonel Alexander Doniphan. They were supposed to pacify the Navajos, and then go through El Paso and Chihuahua City to meet up with General Taylor. Doniphan proceeded to do just that with his group of ragtag volunteer backwoodsmen. This undisciplined gang defeated a much larger Mexican army at El Brazito on Christmas Day 1846. They also won the Battle of the Sacramento near Chihuahua in February of 1847 and then occupied the city.

The "lost" regiment finally met up with Taylor at Saltillo in May of 1847, having marched several thousand miles and won two major victories against larger armies. Most of them took their pay, which they received for the first time in the campaign, and headed home.

Match these people (answers may be used more than once).

2.42	_____ Old Rough and Ready	a.	John Frémont
2.43	_____ army topographer	b.	Zachary Taylor
2.44	_____ victor at Palo Alto and Buena Vista	c.	Alexander Doniphan
2.45	_____ commander, Missouri Mounted Volunteers	d.	Stephen Kearny
2.46	_____ founder of the Bear Flag Republic	e.	Robert Stockton
2.47	_____ captured Santa Fe	f.	Santa Anna
2.48	_____ naval officer, took Los Angeles	g.	James Polk
2.49	_____ Mexican dictator, again		
2.50	_____ captured Matamoros		
2.51	_____ captured Monterrey		
2.52	_____ captured Chihuahua		
2.53	_____ a Jacksonian Democrat		
2.54	_____ victories made Whigs talk of making him president		
2.55	_____ took advantage of Polk's naiveté		

A Growing Nation (1820–1855) | Unit 5

Answer these questions.

2.56 Where were America's superior junior officers of the Mexican War educated?
_____

2.57 The Mexican War provided battle training for the officers of what future war?
_____

2.58 What were two reasons why the Mexican War was controversial?
_____
_____

2.59 Why did Taylor ignore his orders to stay in Monterrey?
_____
_____

2.60 What part of the army contributed decisively to the victories at Palo Alto, Resaca de la Palma, and Buena Vista? _____

Campaign Against Mexico City. General Winfield Scott was the highest-ranking general in the American army during the Mexican War. He was a man who loved pomp, good food, and fancy uniforms. His men called him "Old Fuss and Feathers." He was quick-tempered, touchy, and blunt. He stayed out of the early part of the war because of differences with President Polk. However, he was a brilliant military man, and he proved it in the campaign to capture Mexico City.

In October of 1846, Scott proposed to lead a campaign against the Mexican capital. It was a bold idea. He would have to march from Veracruz on the Gulf of Mexico across miles of poorly mapped, heavily defended territory. He would have to penetrate deep into enemy territory with only a thin supply line. It was a difficult military venture.

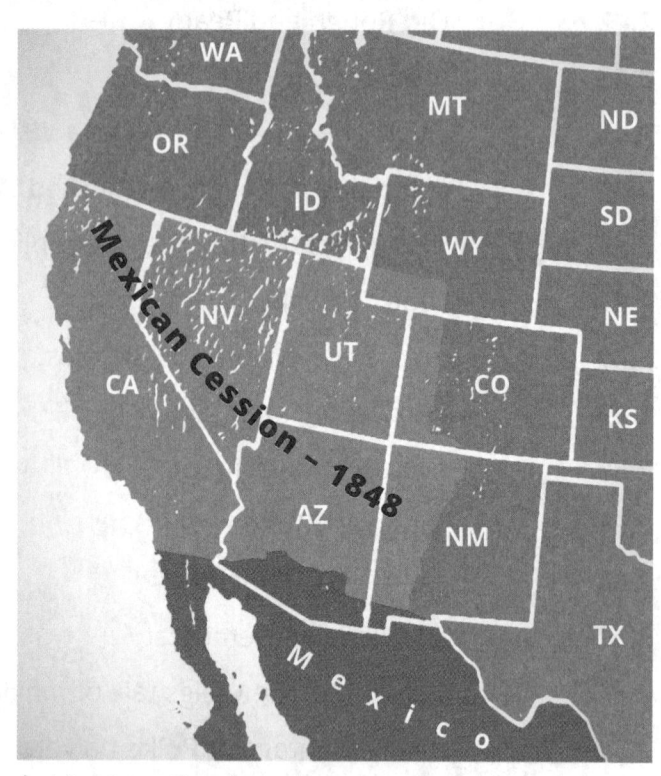

| Mexican Cession

Scott sailed to Mexico with over 10,000 men in 1847. In March he landed his men away from Veracruz and attacked it from the landward side where the defenses were weakest. The siege lasted only a few days. Scott left a small force to occupy the city and moved quickly toward Mexico City.

Santa Anna received word that Scott was coming and went to meet him. The Mexican army set up defenses in a narrow mountain pass near Cerro Gordo. Scott's rapid advance reached the site before the defenses were fully in place. Captain Robert E. Lee, working with the engineers, found and cut a way around the enemy to allow an attack from two sides. The outnumbered Americans won the two-day battle, clearing the road to Mexico City.

At this point, Polk tried again to negotiate the peace he wanted. Nicholas P. Trist, a State Department clerk, was sent to attempt negotiations. The Mexican government refused, but Santa Anna sent a secret offer to Scott. In exchange for $10,000 up front, and $90,000 more after a treaty was signed, Santa Anna would arrange for a treaty that gave the Americans what they wanted. Scott decided to try it and sent the $10,000. The Americans did not get their treaty. Santa Anna pocketed the money and used the time to prepare his defenses.

Scott advanced on the capital in August of 1847. During this part of the campaign, he was cut off from his communications and supplies. He either had to win or surrender. Santa Anna had strong defenses in place to protect the city. Scott took the first of these at Contreras and Churubusco on the 19th and 20th.

The Mexicans then asked for an armistice. Scott granted one for two weeks, believing the enemy wanted to negotiate. Again, Santa Anna used the time to improve his defenses. When the armistice ended, the Americans attacked again, winning a battle at Molino del Rey. They then captured the fortress of Chapultepec which cleared the way right up to the city gates. Santa Anna fled and the city authorities sued for peace. On September 14, 1847, Scott rode into the central plaza of the city and the Stars and Stripes were raised.

Treaty of Guadalupe Hidalgo. Nicholas Trist had been recalled by the president in October. He ignored the order and opened negotiations with the new Mexican government. The two sides met at Guadalupe Hidalgo, a city north of the capital. Faced with an army in their capital, the Mexicans gave the Americans everything they wanted.

The treaty ceded to America all of California and the land between it and Texas north of the Gila River. America agreed to pay 15 million dollars for the land and assume all of Mexico's debts to American citizens for damage claims. Mexico also recognized the Rio Grande as the border of Texas. The treaty was signed on February 2, 1848.

Polk was facing growing pressure to annex all of Mexico. However, when the treaty arrived, the president decided to submit it to the Senate because it gave him what he had originally wanted. He chose to ignore the fact that Trist was not authorized to negotiate for the United States. He may have been motivated by a fear that the government in Mexico would change again and repudiate it. The Senate approved it on March 10.

Results of the War. The Mexican Cession added more than 525,000 square miles (1,360,000 square kilometers) to the nation. It was the largest single piece of land ever to become part of the United States. However, Congress had tremendous difficulty trying to organize the new land into official territories. The sticking point was slavery.

David Wilmot of Pennsylvania had introduced a proposal in 1846, while the war was still in progress. It specified that no slavery would ever be allowed to exist in any land acquired from Mexico as a result of the war. The South fought the Wilmot Proviso with a passion. It passed in the House but failed in the Senate; however, it would not go away. It was introduced repeatedly to acrimonious debate.

After the war, other proposals were offered, some allowing slavery, some forbidding it, and some leaving it up to the citizens of each territory to decide for themselves (popular sovereignty). No agreements could be reached. The issue of organizing the new land hung on the deepening chasm of slavery. It was finally brought to a crisis by the sudden changes that had occurred in California.

California Gold Rush. It was expected that it would be years before any part of the Mexican Cession would have the 60,000 people needed to apply for statehood. However, in 1848, just days before the Treaty of Guadalupe Hidalgo was signed, gold was discovered in the Sierra Nevada Mountains of California. What followed was one of the largest mass migrations in history. Approximately 80,000 people came to California in 1849 hoping to strike it rich. Just about the same number came the next few years. Some left after failing to get rich, but many stayed to make their homes in the West.

The "forty-niners," as they were called, came mainly from the United States by three routes. The largest group came overland via the trading and wagon trails. Another group sailed south to Panama, crossed the Isthmus, and came north by sea to California. Still another group took the difficult ocean route around the southern tip of South America. Hundreds of ships reached the West Coast and were promptly abandoned as all the men aboard went searching for gold. Rotting ships filled San Francisco harbor, which had became a major city overnight.

California's population rapidly exceeded the 60,000 needed for statehood. The official population count in 1850 was over 90,000! In 1849 California organized a government and applied for admission as a state, skipping the intermediate step of territory. The real problem arose because the new state constitution barred slavery. The stage was set for a major sectional battle.

Election of 1848. The Whigs jumped at the chance to run the popular general, Zachary Taylor, for president in 1848. They again bypassed Henry Clay and Daniel Webster, both of whom wanted the nomination. The Democrats nominated General Lewis Cass, a veteran of the War of 1812. President Polk had promised not to run again if he was elected; his health would not permit it in any case. Martin Van Buren ran as a third-party candidate for the anti-slavery Free-Soil Party.

The Whigs and the Democrats avoided the slavery issue. In fact, they avoided most of the issues. The Free-Soil Party, on the other hand, came out openly against slavery in the territories. They also advocated internal improvements and free land for settlers. Their slogan was "free soil, free speech, free labor, and free men." However, it was a contest of personalities, not issues, and the popular Taylor won.

| Gold Prospector by the River

Zachary Taylor. Zachary Taylor (1784-1850) was the son of a wealthy Virginia planter. His father fought in the Revolution, and it was no surprise when Zachary joined the army as a young man. Taylor fought in the Black Hawk and Seminole Indian Wars before becoming a national hero in the Mexican War. He had no political experience and knew very little about national or international affairs. In fact, he had never even voted in a presidential election!

The intense controversy in Congress over the organization of the Mexican Cession was beyond Taylor. He bungled back and forth, unable to resolve the issues. Before any resolution could be worked out, Taylor died in 1850 and Millard Fillmore, his vice president, came to power.

The Last Piece. The growing American population in California and Oregon was causing communication problems. The populated West Coast lands were thousands of miles and months of travel away from the center of government in the East. Several people proposed to build a railroad across the country to connect the two coasts more conveniently.

The most attractive route was across what is now New Mexico and Arizona south of the Gila River. The Rocky Mountains were lower through that part of the West. Unfortunately, that land belonged to Mexico.

In 1853 James Gadsden was sent as the American minister to Mexico. He was authorized to negotiate for the land needed for a railroad route. Gadsden's efforts prospered because Santa Anna was once again (for the sixth time) in power, and the old dictator needed money. He agreed to sell the United States a section of land south of the Gila River for $10 million. The Gadsden Purchase was the last piece of land acquired for what would become the forty-eight contiguous states. Manifest Destiny had been fulfilled.

| Gadsden Purchase

A Growing Nation (1820–1855) | Unit 5

Complete these sentences.

2.61 The Mexican War was ended by the Treaty of _____ .

2.62 The sticking point over organizing the land acquired from Mexico was the issue of _____ .

2.63 Winfield Scott's nickname was _____ .

2.64 California's population grew rapidly after the discovery of _____ in 1848.

2.65 _____ was elected president in 1848.

2.66 Martin Van Buren ran for president in 1848 as a candidate of the _____ Party.

2.67 The last part of the contiguous states added to the Union was the _____ Purchase.

2.68 The men who arrived in California in 1849 were called _____ .

2.69 Winfield Scott led a brilliant campaign that conquered _____ in September of 1847.

2.70 The man who negotiated the treaty that ended the war with Mexico was _____ .

2.71 The three routes to California in the rush after 1848 were:

   a. _____

   b. _____

   c. _____

2.72 America paid _____ dollars to Mexico for the land ceded by them after the war.

2.73 The defense of Mexico City was under the command of the dictator, _____ .

2.74 California organized a government in the year _____ and wanted to become a state without ever being a _____ .

2.75 The slogan of the Free-Soil Party in 1848 was _____ .

2.76 The Gadsden Purchase was made because the U.S. needed the land for a _____ line to the West Coast.

2.77 The two-day battle at the mountain pass near _____ cleared the road to Mexico City for the Americans.

2.78 The land taken from Mexico by the war was called the _____ _____ .

2.79 After the Mexican War, Mexico recognized the _____ as the border of Texas.

2.80 The _____ Proviso that proposed to forbid slavery in land acquired from Mexico did not become law.

2.81 The constitution of California did not allow _____ .

2.82 _____ became president after Taylor died in 1850.

2.83 During the Mexican War, _____ was the highest ranking general in the U.S. army.

Review the material in this section in preparation for the Self Test. This Self Test will check your mastery of this particular section as well as your knowledge of the previous section.

SELF TEST 2

Match these items (each answer, 2 points).

2.01	_____ Wilmot Proviso	a. America should move across the continent, claiming the land
2.02	_____ Missouri Compromise	b. Harrison's presidential campaign
2.03	_____ Tariff of Abominations	c. no petitions on slavery
2.04	_____ Gag Rule	d. Native American removal to west of Mississippi
2.05	_____ *Specie Circular*	e. needed for railroad to the Pacific
2.06	_____ Pet Banks	f. no slavery north of 36° 30'
2.07	_____ Manifest Destiny	g. passed in 1828 to embarrass President Adams, infuriated the South
2.08	_____ Trail of Tears	h. government funds placed there under Jackson
2.09	_____ Log Cabin and Hard Cider	i. no slavery in territory from Mexico
2.010	_____ Gadsden Purchase	j. federal land must be purchased with gold or silver

Name the item or person (each answer, 3 points).

2.011 The three national leaders from the South, West, and North who never became president:

a. _____   b. _____

c. _____

2.012 _____ Name for land acquired after the Mexican War

2.013 _____ Slogan for those who wanted all of Oregon

2.014 _____ One rally cry of the Texas Revolution

2.015 _____ State that was an independent republic for 10 years before joining the Union

2.016 _____ Polk went to war with Mexico to get this state

2.017 _____ The crisis that almost divided the nation under Andrew Jackson

2.018 _____ The "moneyed monster" hated by Jackson and eventually destroyed by him

Unit 5 | **A Growing Nation (1820–1855)**

Answer these questions (each answer, 3 points).

2.019 The United States peacefully resolved border disputes with Great Britain over which two territories in the 1840s?
_____

2.020 How did the Mexican War start?
_____
_____

2.021 What campaign won the Mexican War for America and who led it?
_____
_____

2.022 What happened at the Alamo in 1836?
_____
_____
_____

2.023 What were Zachary Taylor's qualifications for president?
_____
_____

2.024 What were the terms of the Treaty of Guadalupe Hidalgo?
_____
_____
_____

2.025 What was the "corrupt bargain" that Jackson claimed John Quincy Adams used to win the presidency?
_____
_____

2.026 Why could Congress not agree on organizing the new territories after the Mexican War?
_____
_____

A Growing Nation (1820–1855) | Unit 5

2.027 Why was James Polk chosen as the Democratic candidate for president?
_____
_____

2.028 What happened to the Democratic-Republican Party after the election of John Quincy Adams?
_____
_____

Match these people (each answer, 2 points).

2.029	_____ became president at Harrison's death, a Whig with Democrat ideas	a.	Andrew Jackson
2.030	_____ brilliant American general, highest-ranking officer during Mexican War	b.	Sam Houston
		c.	William H. Harrison
2.031	_____ served in House of Representatives for years after presidency	d.	Henry Clay
		e.	James K. Polk
2.032	_____ the Great Compromiser	f.	Zachary Taylor
2.033	_____ hero of New Orleans, the people's president	g.	Winfield Scott
		h.	Martin Van Buren
2.034	_____ Jackson's hand-picked successor, the Little Magician	i.	John Quincy Adams
		j.	John Tyler
2.035	_____ victor at Buena Vista, Old Rough and Ready		
2.036	_____ Texan, victor at San Jacinto against Santa Anna		
2.037	_____ added more territory to the Union than any other president		
2.038	_____ president for only 31 days		

80 / 100   SCORE _____   TEACHER _____ _____
                                      initials   date

50 | Section 2

3. GROWTH AND DIVISION

America grew in the early 1800s in more than just size. The Industrial Revolution brought manufacturing growth which would eventually make America a world power. Innovations in transportation, agriculture, manufacturing, and communications caused unprecedented changes in American life. Trade grew and the various parts of the frontier were brought into the national economy as transport became easier. Life became easier as machines took over backbreaking manual labor. The new industries created large pools of wealth that further fed the growth of industry and commerce.

American life also saw changes as immigration brought in large numbers of new citizens.

A revival broke out in the early 1800s that led thousands to the Lord. A reform movement followed the revival and touched many areas of American life.

The great tragedy of the era was the continuation of slavery and the South's stubborn defense of it. The Kansas-Nebraska Act destroyed the Missouri Compromise and much of the remaining trust between the anti-slavery North and the pro-slavery South. The anti-slavery Republican Party was formed and leaped onto the national scene. The breakup of the Union was drawing near.

SECTION OBJECTIVES

Review these objectives. When you have completed this section, you should be able to:

1. Name the leaders of the era and explain their accomplishments.
3. Trace the development of the slavery and tariff issues from 1820 to 1855.
4. Define Manifest Destiny and describe its course in America.
6. Define the Industrial Revolution and name the people, innovations, and inventions that contributed to it.
7. Describe the effects of the Industrial Revolution in America.
8. Describe the Second Great Awakening and the reform movements that followed it.
9. Describe the compromises that kept the nation together and what ended them.
10. Describe the changes in America and American life in this era.

VOCABULARY

Study these words to enhance your learning success in this section.

comptroller (komp trō' ler). A public official who audits government accounts.

denomination (di nom i nā' shun). A religious organization uniting in a single administrative body a number of local congregations.

heresy (her' e sē). A belief different from the standard beliefs of the church.

patent (pat' nt). A document that gives an inventor the sole right to make, use or sell his invention for so many years.

platform (plat' form). Statement of policies and ideas adopted by a political party.

polygamy (po lig′ a mē). Marriage to more than one person at one time, usually the taking of several wives by one man.

propaganda (prop a gan′ da). The spreading of ideas or information for the purpose of helping or injuring a cause, institution, or person.

temperance (tem′ pe rens). Moderation in or abstinence from the use of intoxicating drinks.

The Industrial Revolution

Not all revolutions are violent. Second only to the War for Independence, the greatest revolution in American history was the Industrial Revolution. This revolution was the change from a farming and handcrafting society to one of industry and machine manufacturing. It began in England in the 1700s and eventually spread to reach much of the world. It began in America, in a small way, late in that same century, but it did not become an important part of American culture until the War of 1812. It was the embargoes and blockades of that war that pushed American manufacturing to begin its spectacular rise.

Textiles. The revolution had its most successful beginning in the textile industry. Britain had developed many of the machines used in the mass production of cloth in the late 1700s. These machines spun several spools of yarn or thread instead of the one at a time that could be done by hand. British inventors had also invented the power loom that allowed cloth to be woven more quickly. These inventions were protected by laws that prohibited plans of the machines or people who knew them from leaving the country.

However, the laws did not stop Samuel Slater, the "Father of the Factory System (in America). Slater was a skilled mechanic familiar with the British textile machines. He memorized the plans for the machines and succeeded in reaching the United States in disguise. In 1791 with the financial backing of Moses Brown, a New England capitalist, Slater opened America's first factory for spinning thread in Rhode Island.

The new factory was opened in time to cash in on the flood of cotton from the South. Eli Whitney invented the cotton gin in 1793, allowing for the cheap production of this textile fiber. The factories of the North were soon busy turning Southern cotton into cotton thread. These same factories began to weave it into cloth when the power loom was added to the American system in 1814. The textile industry received another boost in 1846 when Elias Howe **patented** the sewing machine. It was further perfected by Isaac Singer who made it popular. It was the first in a long line of labor-saving devices that began to appear

| Cotton Gin

in American homes, not just factories. It also allowed the factories to begin mass-producing clothes from their inexpensive thread and cloth.

Most of the factories were located in the northeast for several reasons. The machines were powered at first by water wheels that required fast-moving streams. The steep hills and swift streams of New England were ideal for these kinds of factories. The poor soil of New England encouraged people to try the alternative of manufacturing. Northern seaports provided a ready way to bring in raw material and export finished goods. New England also had a ready supply of capital from its many wealthy shipping entrepreneurs. Moreover, the northeast was the most densely populated part of the nation, providing the factories with needed workers. The West, by contrast, was sparsely populated by poor farmers, and the South was populated by rich plantation owners whose money was in cotton and slaves.

Mass Production. Eli Whitney made very little money on his cotton gin. He obtained a patent for the device, but others still produced the simple machine. By the time Whitney had gone through the courts and put the illegal manufacturers out of business, his patent had almost expired, so he had to earn his fortune another way. The way he chose once again revolutionized American manufacturing.

Whitney came up with the idea of mass production of interchangeable parts for guns. Prior to that time, each part of a gun was made by hand and it fit only that particular gun. If a part broke, a new one had to be handmade to replace it. Whitney had the parts made in large groups, each exactly alike. That way, a broken part could be easily and quickly replaced. The guns could be manufactured and maintained at a lesser cost. Whitney reportedly proved his point by taking ten guns to Washington for government officials to see. He took them apart, scrambled the pieces, and reassembled them into ten working guns!

Mass production of interchangeable parts spread to all areas of manufacturing. The cheap production of many goods brought those goods within reach for more and more people. It also gave the North a vast manufacturing engine that would be vital in the coming war with the South.

Factory Workers. The factory system was very beneficial to the nation by providing new jobs, cheaper goods, and economic prosperity; but it also had a downside. Many factory workers were shamefully exploited. Wages were low and hours were long. Thirteen- or fourteen-hour days, six days a week were common. Unions were considered conspiracies, and strikes for better pay often were broken up by the law. Working conditions were bad and often unsafe. An injured or ill worker had no protection from losing their job.

The worst abuse was the employment of children in the factories. Children, often under the age of ten, were put to work tending the machines for pitiful wages. They worked the same hours as the adults, deprived of their childhood and frequently their health by years of labor. Working also meant they could not get an education, and that often meant they would be unskilled laborers for all their lives. This child abuse was one of the blackest marks on the growth of industry in America and would continue for many years.

Gradually, improvements were made. Martin Van Buren set a precedent in 1840 when he limited workers on federal projects to ten hours a day. Slowly, the states began to pass laws limiting working hours. In 1842 the Supreme Court ruled that labor unions were not automatically illegal conspiracies. However, it would be many years before unions could build up the strength to effectively challenge the power of the employers.

Farming. Farming also profited from the Industrial Revolution. The thickly matted soil of the West had been hard on the heavy wooden plows that existed in the 1700s. In 1837 John Deere invented a light, sharp steel plow for western farmers. A few years earlier, Cyrus McCormick had patented a mechanical reaper. This remarkable invention allowed a man to harvest his grain by himself faster than he could with several helpers.

The new plow and reaper allowed a farmer to produce substantially more food than he needed for his family. Suddenly, farming was not just a way to survive, it was a way to make a profit!! Fertile western farms began to supply food for cotton-growing southern plantations and cotton-spinning northern factories. The different parts of the country specialized and depended upon the others for what they did not produce themselves.

Communication. The single greatest revolution in the history of communication was the invention of the telegraph by Samuel Morse. Morse invented a way to send messages instantly over a wire using a series of dots and dashes called Morse Code. In 1844 he sent a message from Washington to Baltimore, "What hath God wrought?" opening the era of instant communications! Soon, telegraph wires were all over the nation, allowing news and information to speed across the American expanse. In 1866 after five failures, Cyrus Field succeeded in laying a telegraph cable between Canada and Great Britain. The Old and New World were suddenly just a few seconds apart.

| McCormick's Reaper advertisement, the caption read, "The People's Favorite! The World-Renowned McCormick Twine Binder! Victorious in over 100 Field Trials! New and Valuable Improvements for 1884!"

Match these people (some answers will be used more than once).

3.1 _____ Father of the Factory System   a. Cyrus McCormick
3.2 _____ cotton gin   b. Cyrus Field
3.3 _____ interchangeable parts for guns   c. John Deere
3.4 _____ invented the telegraph   d. Elias Howe
3.5 _____ opened America's first thread-spinning factory   e. Eli Whitney
3.6 _____ invented the sewing machine   f. Isaac Singer
3.7 _____ steel plow   g. Samuel Morse
3.8 _____ improved and popularized the sewing machine   h. Samuel Slater
3.9 _____ "What hath God wrought?"
3.10 _____ mechanical reaper
3.11 _____ memorized British machine plans and came to America
3.12 _____ laid a telegraph cable from Europe to North America

Complete the following.

3.13 Where did the worldwide Industrial Revolution begin? _____

3.14 How did the new farm machines change Western farming?
_____

3.15 Name three reasons why factories developed in the Northeast.
   a. _____
   b. _____
   c. _____

3.16 Name four ways the factory system exploited workers.
   a. _____
   b. _____
   c. _____
   d. _____

3.17 What was the Industrial Revolution?
_____
_____

Transportation Needs. Improvements in transportation were a vital part of the Industrial Revolution. At the time of the American Revolution, transportation was very poor. Roads were unpaved, muddy, rutted, and often impassable for wagons. The most reliable transportation was by water, but the rivers did not go to every farm. Since most farms produced only for the needs of the family, it was not a vital concern until the Industrial Revolution. However, before farms could provide food for cities devoted to manufacturing, they needed reliable ways to ship their produce.

Roads. The first improvements in overland transportation came through privately owned turnpikes at the end of the 1700s. The Lancaster Turnpike was a pioneer in this field. It was a wide road with a hard surface and was built by a private company. The company made a substantial profit charging tolls for commerce between Philadelphia and Lancaster, Pennsylvania. Its success encouraged many other companies to invest in these arteries. Commerce flourished along these routes, encouraging more of the same.

The Cumberland Road, also called the National Road, was built with public funds. It ran from Cumberland, Maryland to Vandalia, Illinois (completed in 1852). Connecting roads made it a fairly direct route between Baltimore on Chesapeake Bay, and St. Louis on the Mississippi River. It was a huge stimulant to trade, western migration, and the development of the cities of the frontier.

However, public roads were difficult to build. It was very expensive to build roads in the middle of the wilderness, miles from major sources of supplies, manpower, and food. States' rights advocates, like the Democrats, objected violently to using federal funds for any project inside one state. Moreover, the Northeast did not want to aid roads that would encourage their population to move west. So, additions to the national road that would connect it with major cities in Kentucky, for example, were routinely voted down or vetoed, especially by Andrew Jackson. Nevertheless, with dedicated state spending, the hard-surface roads were gradually expanded.

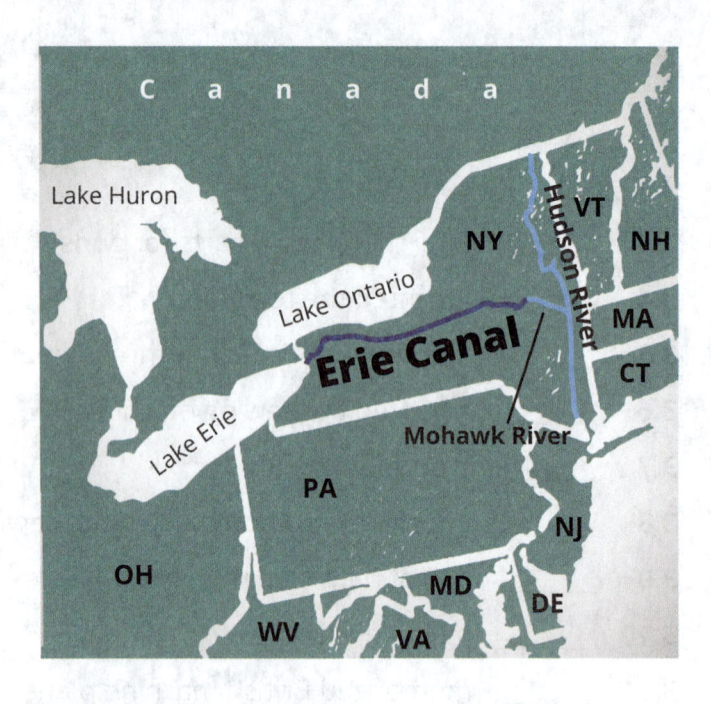

The Steamboat. The mighty rivers of America, especially the Mississippi, were major trade routes. However, prior to 1807 they were basically one-way streets. Shipping goods downstream from a farm in Illinois to New Orleans, for example, was slow but simple. A farmer only had to build a raft and float it carefully down the river. However, going upstream carrying cargo of any bulk was incredibly difficult and too expensive to be very profitable.

That all changed in 1807 when Robert Fulton built a workable steamboat. It used a steam engine (which had been invented by other people) to drive a paddle wheel on the side of the ship. Fulton's ship, the *Clermont*, was called "Fulton's Folly" by his detractors. No one was laughing, however, when the ship steamed up the Hudson River from New York City to Albany in 32 hours—an unheard-of feat!

The steamboats rapidly spread to all the navigable rivers of the nation. They especially came to dominate trade on the Mississippi where a thousand or more people were working by 1860. Cities along the upper reaches of the river flourished as trade expanded. The Supreme Court decision of *Gibbons v. Ogden* in 1824 prohibited the states from controlling interstate trade on these rivers. That opened up these vital routes to healthy competition and rapid expansion.

Canal Craze. Even with better roads, water transportation was still better for large quantities of bulky cargo, but the rivers did not connect many of the vital inland water routes. This problem was corrected by a surge of canal building in the early 1800s.

The most famous and most successful of the internal canals was the Erie Canal in New York State. The Erie Canal connected Lake Erie with the Atlantic Ocean through the Mohawk and Hudson Rivers. It was promoted by New York Governor DeWitt Clinton. The federal government would not contribute any funds, so the difficult project was built entirely with New York money. Clinton's opponents called it "Clinton's Ditch." The determined governor persevered from 1817 until 1825, when the canal finally opened.

The canal was an unprecedented success. The time required to ship a ton of grain from Buffalo to New York City fell from twenty days to six days, and the cost dropped from $100 to $5! The Erie Canal connected New York City to the entire Midwest by the Great Lakes. The city quickly became the premier port on the eastern seaboard because of the influx of produce from the West. Land values along the canal shot up. Industry flourished with a ready source of raw materials and a cheap method for shipping out finished goods. "Clinton's Ditch" was New York's gold mine!

Other states observed the success and tried to copy it. A flurry of canal construction occurred in the 1820s and '30s. Several canals were built to connect the Mississippi and the Great Lakes. This also benefitted the trade going into New York City via the Erie Canal. One of the most unusual canals connected the Susquehanna River above Chesapeake Bay to the Ohio River; it used a special railroad to lift the barges over the Allegheny Mountains. Many of these canals were a commercial success for a short time, but none rivaled the economic impact of the Erie Canal.

Ocean Trade. The steamboats and canals brought American products to seaports for trade with the world. America led the world in the mid-1800s in the development of a new ocean vessel, the clipper ship. Clipper ships were streamlined vessels built with a huge collection of sails. They were built for speed, not bulk, to carry valuable cargoes quickly. They quickly took over the tea trade to the Far East and were the vessel of choice for the impatient thousands heading to the California gold fields.

However, the majestic clippers were put out of business by the development of ocean-going steamships. These unlovely, slower ships were reliable and could carry much more cargo. By the time of the Civil War, the beautiful clippers were losing their cargoes to the cheaper transport of the smoke-belching steamers.

Railroad. The success of the canals was quickly ended by the incredible story of the railroads. These speedy monsters could go anywhere tracks could be laid. They were not dependent upon waterways or limited by hills and mountains. Railroads could carry bulky cargo even to cities that had no nearby river or lake.

Rail lines were used in the early 1800s to connect major cities using horse-drawn coaches. It was in Britain that the newly developed steam engine was first adapted to pull these coaches. It was also in Britain that the standard gauge (rail separation) of 4 feet 8 1/2 inches was set. (This was the standard width for wagon axles in Britain because the deep ruts in the old Roman roads were that distance apart. It had been the width of Roman chariot axles and became the railroad width in Britain, Canada, and the United States!)

A Growing Nation (1820–1855) | Unit 5

The first American company to try the new technology was the Baltimore and Ohio Company which began service in 1830 with thirteen miles of track. That same year the B&O publicized its new venture by staging a race between a horse-drawn rail coach and one drawn by the *Tom Thumb*, an American-built locomotive. The *Tom Thumb* was winning until it broke down and the horse crossed the finish line first. It did not matter—the railroad had arrived.

The railroad expanded rapidly and quickly took up a vital role in the nation. From the thirteen miles set up by the B&O in 1830, the rail lines grew to about 30,000 miles by 1860! Most of these tracks were in the industrial North and the rapidly expanding West around the Great Lakes. The railroad gave the farmers of Ohio, Illinois, and Indiana direct access to the markets of the northeast. This vital river of iron replaced the Mississippi as the main trade route of the West. That stopped the South from choking off the West by their control of the Mississippi seaports during the Civil War.

| Early Steam Locomotive

Answer these questions.

3.18 Why was better transportation needed for the Industrial Revolution?
_____
_____

3.19 Why didn't the federal government build more roads?
_____
_____

3.20 Why was the railroad important to the West in the Civil War?
_____
_____

3.21 Why were so many canals built in the years after 1825?

_____

_____

3.22 What put the clipper ships out of business?

_____

Match these items (some answers will be used more than once).

3.23	_____ *Gibbons v. Ogden* gave these unfettered competition	a.	steamboats
3.24	_____ built by private companies that made a profit on tolls	b.	clipper ships
3.25	_____ *Clermont*	c.	turnpikes
3.26	_____ *Tom Thumb's* owners	d.	railroads
3.27	_____ had 30,000 miles by 1860	e.	canals
3.28	_____ made New York City the most important Eastern port	f.	Erie Canal
3.29	_____ the National Road	g.	Cumberland Road
3.30	_____ major land artery between Chesapeake Bay and the Mississippi	h.	Baltimore and Ohio
3.31	_____ took over the tea trade with the Far East because of their speed		
3.32	_____ dropped the cost of shipping a ton of grain from Buffalo to New York City from $100 to $5		
3.33	_____ ocean vessels built for speed		
3.34	_____ made the rivers into two-way streets		
3.35	_____ first railroad in the U.S.		
3.36	_____ pioneer connected Lancaster and Philadelphia		
3.37	_____ Clinton's Ditch		
3.38	_____ connected Mississippi River and Great Lakes		
3.39	_____ one used to connect the Susquehanna and Ohio Rivers and used a railroad to get over the Allegheny Mountains		
3.40	_____ its success ended the success of canals		
3.41	_____ transport for large quantities of bulk cargo, did not require waterways		

Changing American Life

Immigration. The population of the United States continued to grow at a remarkable rate in the early 1800s. Since colonial times, the population had continued to double every 23 years! By 1860 America had the fourth-largest national population in the world. Much of this was due to the country's remarkable birthrate; but by the early 1800s, the native-born citizens were being supplemented by immigrants from Europe. The rate of immigration skyrocketed in the 1840s, primarily from Ireland and Germany.

Ireland was a land held in near slavery by Great Britain. In order to feed their families, the Irish peasants were forced to rent land from British landlords. British law restricted the rights of Catholics who made up most of the Irish population. The last straw was the Potato Famine from 1845-1847. The Irish people lived on potatoes and in those years the crops were destroyed by a blight. An estimated 2 million people died of starvation and disease. Boatloads of Irishmen left their homeland out of desperation. Hundreds of thousands came to America during those bleak years.

Irish immigrants were too poor to buy land and supplies. They could not move west; therefore, they tended to congregate in the cities of the East Coast. They had little education and quickly filled the ranks of the unskilled laborers. Many found work building the canals and railroads. They often lived in filthy city tenements and faced death from the diseases bred by poor sanitation. Moreover, the Catholic Irish were distrusted by the more established Protestant Americans. They were often denied jobs because of their ancestry. "No Irish Need Apply" was a common note added to a job offer.

The concentration of Irish immigrants in the cities slowly built their political power. Politicians found it necessary to cater to the "Irish vote." Some Irish, notably Tammany Hall in New York City, built extensive political control organizations called "machines" that literally controlled the city. Irishmen came to dominate the police and fire departments of many Northeastern cities. In time, the Irish found a piece of the American pie.

The other large group of immigrants came from Germany. Most of these people were farmers displaced by hard times or political upheaval. A few of the immigrants were intellectuals who fled in 1848 after revolutions for greater freedom failed in Europe. As with the Irish, hundreds of thousands of German immigrants came in the 1800s. Unlike the Irish, the German newcomers usually had some money. As a result, they did not stay in the eastern cities. They moved west, often to the northern states of the upper Mississippi River, such as Wisconsin and Michigan. They built prosperous farms and integrated into American life. They brought their love of *bier* (beer) and their brewing skills to their new homeland, as well as their tradition of hard work.

Know-Nothing Party. The 1840s and '50s saw a rise of anti-immigrant feelings in America. The sudden influx of Irish and German people alarmed native-born Americans. The poverty of many of the immigrants left them dependent on charity and public support. Many of the newcomers were also Catholic, and anti-Catholicism was still strong in the United States. Several incidents of anti-Catholic violence occurred in the mid-1800s. The strongest evidence of the anti-immigrant sentiment was the creation of the Know-Nothing Party.

The Know-Nothing Party developed from the Order of the Star Spangled Banner, created in 1849. It was a political organization that called for strict control on immigration, deportation of poor immigrants, and long waiting periods for citizenship and the right to vote. It was called the Know-Nothing Party because of its secrecy. Its rally cry was "America for the Americans."

The party won several elections on the local and state level in the 1850s, but they were never able to successfully push their agenda. The controversy over slavery split the movement and ended its day of glory. It disappeared after a dismal showing in the 1856 elections.

The Second Great Awakening. In the 1730s and '40s, The Great Awakening had turned the hearts of many of the American colonists to God. Revival struck the nation again in the late 1790s. This visitation of God's Spirit was called the Second Great Awakening, and it lasted into the 1830s. This revival did not have the prominent leaders the first one had with George Whitefield and Jonathan Edwards. It also was less intense, but it lasted longer and covered a larger area.

The fervor of American Christianity had gone cold in the years since the Great Awakening. The spread of the frontier had taken people further and further from organized churches. The needs of survival had drawn hearts away from God, and the roughness of frontier life had pushed aside the Savior's gentle touch. However, the preachers of the early 1800s found a way to reach the scattered masses of the frontier: the camp meeting.

Camp meetings were large gatherings of people to hear several days of preaching and teaching from the Word of God. The place was advertised in advance, and people would come from all over the region and camp at the site. Hundreds and sometimes thousands of people would attend. People were attracted to the meetings by a chance to socialize and to enjoy some stimulation in their monotonous wilderness lives. They often came away changed by the message of Christ's love and salvation.

The camp meeting revivals were often extremely emotional. People would sing, dance, shout, and shake. Salvation was often accompanied by hysterical weeping and repenting. The emotionalism was criticized by many, and some preachers tried to control it.

| A Circuit-Riding Preacher

The revival eventually spread to the cities due to the work of traveling evangelists who came out of the Awakening. The most famous was Charles Finney who preached to large crowds in the cities in the 1820s to the 1850s. Finney saw a great mass of people turn to God in New York City where he primarily worked. Another great city evangelist was D. L. Moody who worked out of Chicago beginning in the 1850s. Moody went on to found the Moody Bible Institute in that city. Both men concentrated on preaching individual salvation and the Bible as the Word of God.

The Methodists and Baptists which welcomed greater emotionalism were the **denominations** that grew the most during this revival. The new congregations were served by "circuit riders," pastors who traveled hundreds of miles visiting each church on his circuit in turn. The most renowned of these traveling pastors was Francis Asbury (1745-1816), who was the leader of the American Methodist Church. He traveled thousands of miles a year on horseback, via frontier roads or trails to serve the people under his care.

Other Sects. Other sects developed in the 1800s which most evangelical Christians would call **heresies**. The deist tradition of the founding fathers led to the development of Unitarianism in the early 1800s. This belief stripped the gospel of the doctrines of sin, grace, and salvation. Unitarians believed there was no trinity, only one God, hence the name *Unitarian*. They also said that Jesus was not God, man was essentially good, and good works were the way to "salvation." Thus, man needed only himself, not God.

Another prominent sect was the Church of Jesus Christ of Latter-Day Saints (Mormons). The Mormon religion was founded in the 1830s by Joseph Smith. Smith claimed to have had a vision in which an angel told him to dig up some golden plates written in an ancient language. Given a way to translate the tablets, Smith claimed to have written the Book of Mormon from them. This book is the basis of Mormon beliefs.

The Mormon religion began in Missouri, and later Smith and his followers moved to Illinois. They were distrusted and persecuted there. Eventually, Smith was murdered and most of his followers left under the leadership of Brigham Young. Young led the group to the dry, empty wilderness of Utah to allow them to live in peace and follow their own ways, which included **polygamy**.

In the mid-1800s, the well-organized Mormons irrigated and built the state into a prosperous community. The number of believers grew due to high birthrates and aggressive missionary work. The powerful hierarchy of the church clashed with the federal government when the population grew large enough to allow a territory to be organized. Much of the conflict centered on the practice of polygamy, which traditional Christians found repulsive. Eventually, the Mormons gave up that practice, and Utah was allowed to become a state in 1896.

| Carrie Nation, a colorful Temperance Leader

Reform Movements. The revival of Christianity caused a renewed interest in reforms. The reform movement dealt with prisons, treatment of the insane, debt law, drinking, working conditions, and women's rights. In the early 1800s, many laws were passed reforming problems in these areas. Imprisonment for debt was gradually ended. Brutal forms of punishment like whipping and branding were eliminated. The concept of trying to reform, not just punish, criminals was introduced. This was especially applied to young children drawn into a life of crime. Improvements were made in the brutal treatment of the insane. Dorthea Dix led the way in this area, traveling all over the nation publicizing the way insane people were caged and tied like animals.

The **temperance** movement also gained force in this time period. Heavy drinking was an American tradition, especially on the frontier. It came under increasing attacks by reformers as Christianity reasserted itself. Men were encouraged to "take the pledge," which was an oath never to drink again. Thousands did so in well-organized temperance rallies. The movement also made good use of public advertisements on the evils of drinking.

The campaign for women's rights also began in the early 1800s. At that time, women could not vote, all of their property belonged to their husbands, and the husbands were even free to beat them, to a certain extent. The movement for women's rights grew out of women participating in the abolitionist movement. The political activism of that cause led many women to question why they were denied full protection of the law and the right to vote.

The official beginning of the modern movement for women's rights was at the Seneca Falls Convention. A few of the pioneers of the women's movement met at the Convention in 1848 and drew up a statement of rights for women. It was based on the Declaration of Independence, declaring that "all men *and* women are created equal." It drew a tremendous amount of ridicule in the press. Many of the original supporters backed away from it, but the women would not be silenced. Gradually, colleges began to admit women, and laws were passed giving them rights to their own property. However, it would be many years before legal equality was achieved.

Another important movement was the growing support for public education. Massachusetts had led the way in colonial times, but education was primarily a privilege of the rich through the 1700s. The situation began to change with the expansion of the right to vote. Poor working men who voted began to demand education for their children. Gradually the wealthy members of society began to realize the advantages of having education available to all, preventing illiterate voters from controlling the elections. The idea that good citizens need to be educated pushed the state governments to pay for elementary education for everyone. Reformers also created better textbooks and set up training schools for teachers.

The most noticeable reform movement of the early to mid-1800s was the abolitionist movement. The case for eliminating slavery had been gaining momentum for years. Slavery was abolished in Great Britain in 1833, thanks to the impressive labor of William Wilberforce, a wealthy evangelical Christian. This freed the slaves in the nearby British West Indies and encouraged the movement in America.

Moderate abolitionists wanted to end slavery slowly, possibly with compensation for slave owners. They hoped to use moral persuasion and increasingly anti-slavery laws to end the institution. This had been the successful pattern in Britain, but Britain did not have a place like the southern United States.

It was the extreme abolitionists who attracted the most attention, however. They were led by William Garrison who founded the anti-slavery newspaper, *The Liberator,* in 1831. Garrison condemned slavery in violent terms that disturbed more moderate abolitionists. He received many death threats and was attacked by mobs several times while giving speeches that presented his views. He continued to publish the newspaper until 1865 which was when the 13th amendment to the Constitution was ratified by the states and slavery officially ended.

Another man who for a short time also published a newspaper that supported the anti-slavery movement was Elijah P. Lovejoy. His presses were repeatedly destroyed, and he was eventually killed by a mob in 1837. The death of Lovejoy gave the anti-slavery movement their first martyr.

Men like Garrison and Lovejoy caused reactions of fear and hatred in the South. Southerners defended their peculiar institution all the more. They argued that their slaves were part of their families and better off than poor factory workers in the North. The two sides found it increasingly difficult even to discuss the issue, much less reach agreement on it.

A Growing Nation (1820–1855) | Unit 5

Complete these sentences.

3.42 The _____ was a Christian revival from the 1790s to the 1830s.

3.43 The _____ Party was a political party that was anti-immigrant.

3.44 The two largest groups of immigrants in the early 1800s came from _____ and _____ .

3.45 Mormons got into trouble with the government largely over the practice of _____ .

3.46 Many Irishmen came to America because of the _____ in 1845-1847.

3.47 The frontier revivals of the early 1800s were spread by means of large, emotional _____ .

3.48 The modern women's rights movement began at the _____ _____ in 1848.

3.49 _____ believe in only one God, not a Trinity, and that man is good.

3.50 Extreme abolitionist William Garrison started the newspaper, _____ , in 1831.

3.51 The _____ movement used ads and pledges to reduce drinking in America.

3.52 The creator of Mormonism was _____ .

3.53 _____ was largely responsible for ending slavery in Great Britain.

3.54 The two denominations that grew most from the revivals of the early 1800s were the _____ and the _____ .

3.55 _____ led the Mormons out of Illinois to form their own community in what would become the state of _____ .

3.56 Six of the areas that reformers tried to change in the early 1800s were.
_____ , _____ ,
_____ , _____ ,
_____ , and _____ .

Answer true or false.

3.57 _____ Circuit riders were pastors of several churches spread over a large area.

3.58 _____ Irish immigrants were usually very poor.

3.59 _____ German immigrants tended to stay in the cities of the Northeast.

3.60 _____ The reform movements were partly a result of the Second Great Awakening.

3.61 _____ D. L. Moody was the early leader of the American Methodist Church.

3.62 _____ Moderate abolitionists wanted to end slavery immediately.

3.63 _____ America in the early 1800s was generally anti-Catholic.

3.64 _____ "America for the Americans," was the rally cry of Dorthea Dix.

3.65 _____ *The Book of Mormon* was supposedly taken from the words spoken by an angel to Brigham Young.

3.66 _____ D. L. Moody was an evangelist who worked out of Chicago.

The Great Divide

Last Compromise. California opened a hornet's nest when it requested admission into the Union in 1849. The Union had exactly fifteen slave and fifteen free states at the time. That meant the South could block any anti-slavery laws by its control of half of the votes in the Senate. Loss of that veto power was a serious threat to the South, or so they believed. The South was not about to lose it without a fight, and the Union was again threatened. Into the gap stepped the old giants: Clay, Webster, and Calhoun, for their last major appearance on the public stage. All of them would be dead by 1852. Clay, "the Great Compromiser," proposed a series of laws that would save the Union. Calhoun opposed them, but died before the debate concluded. Webster spoke strongly in support of compromise for the sake of the country, a stand that brought him heavy condemnation from abolitionists. Eventually, a compromise was worked out and accepted by the nation, with a sigh of relief.

The Compromise of 1850 was a series of agreements that tried to balance each other. The first allowed California to join the Union as a free state. That permanently cost the South its veto in the Senate. In exchange, slavery would not be barred in the remaining states in the Mexican Cession. They would have popular sovereignty on the issue of slavery (chosen for themselves).

The state of Texas claimed a large piece of territory that is now part of the states of New Mexico, Colorado, Wyoming, Kansas and Oklahoma. That land was taken from Texas. In exchange, Texas received $10 million in compensation.

The moderate abolitionists had been trying for years to restrict or eliminate slavery in Washington D.C. as a step on their agenda of gradual abolition. The Compromise gave them an end to the slave trade, but not slavery, in the American capital. The South was also given a much stronger fugitive slave act because of the many concessions they made.

The Fugitive Slave Act of 1850 was something the South had wanted for a long time. For many years abolitionists had been running the "Underground Railroad" to help enslaved people escape to Canada. The Railroad was actually a series of houses on the road north, called "stations," where slaves could hide and receive help to reach the next stop. People who helped on the route were called "conductors" and the escaping slaves "passengers." One remarkable conductor, Harriet Tubman, herself an escaped slave, returned to the South repeatedly and led over 300 people to freedom on the Railroad.

The Underground Railroad infuriated the South. Only a small percentage of enslaved people escaped that way, but it was the principle that grated on slave owners. In their eyes, their property was being stolen by a well-organized conspiracy and the officials in the North were not doing anything to stop it. Southerners had been arguing for a stronger federal law to stop the "thefts." They got it as part of the Compromise of 1850.

The law regarding fugitive slaves was harsh. A black person who was accused of being a runaway slave could not testify in their own behalf or post bail, nor would the case be heard by a jury. The commissioner who decided the case was paid five dollars if the prisoner was released and ten dollars if they were not, a practice that sounded very much like a bribe. Federal officials were required to act as slave catchers. Any private person who aided an escaping slave or refused to aid in their capture was subject to fines or imprisonment.

The law was a serious mistake. It caused many people who had not opposed slavery to become abolitionists and many moderates to become extremists. The injustices of the law inflamed the North. Free black people who were captured by "slave catchers" had no possible way to prove they were not slaves. Escaped slaves who had lived in the North for years were sent back to angry masters. Honest men who opposed slavery and helped their fellow man reach freedom went to jail or lost their worldly wealth for helping them. The people of the North now saw the effects of slavery in their own towns and cities. Southerners became increasingly frustrated as the law was ignored, avoided, and condemned.

| Underground Railroad

The reaction in the North was strong. Mobs freed slaves who were taken under the Fugitive Slave Act. At times, troops had to be used to guard black captives and escort them south. Northern states tried to hamper the law by refusing to aid federal officials and denying the use of state jails. "The Bloodhound Bill" or the "Man-Stealing Law," as it was called, was opposed in print all over the North. The law did a great deal to unify the North and lay the ground work for the Civil War.

Millard Fillmore. Millard Fillmore (1800-1874) became president in 1850 when Zachary Taylor died. Fillmore was born in New York. He had been apprenticed to a cloth maker as a boy but eventually went into the practice of law in his home state. He served in the House of Representatives in New York and Washington. He was serving as **comptroller** of New York when he was chosen to run with Zachary Taylor. Since Taylor was from the South, a New Yorker was added to balance the Whig ticket to represent the whole nation.

Fillmore was a good friend and follower of Henry Clay. He had presided over the Senate as vice president during the debates on the Compromise of 1850. He favored the Compromise even though Taylor opposed it and had threatened to veto it, so Fillmore put his new administration firmly behind the bills, which were stalled in Congress. The Compromise passed and Fillmore signed it. It was the one significant accomplishment of his presidency, and it preserved the Union for ten more years.

Election of 1852. By 1852, Northern opposition to the Fugitive Slave Law had divided the Whig party. Fillmore, who supported the law, did not get the nomination. Instead, the Whigs relied on one of their favorite tricks, nominating a war hero. In this case, they nominated Winfield Scott, "Old Fuss and Feathers," the brilliant commander of the campaign against Mexico City. Their **platform** supported the Compromise of 1850 even though Scott opposed slavery. The Whigs were badly split because the Northerners hated the party platform.

The Democrats were also divided and wound up nominating a "dark horse" candidate, Franklin Pierce. Pierce was a pro-slavery northerner who warmly supported all of the Compromise of 1850. Other than that, Pierce and Scott were both distinguished by their lack of controversial stands on any issues. However, Scott's personal stand against slavery and his pompous nature cost him the election. The slavery issue had successfully split the Whigs. Their party was nearing extinction.

Franklin Pierce. Franklin Pierce (1804-1869) won the Democratic nomination only after the four primary candidates had fought to a draw at the convention. Pierce was born to a wealthy family in New Hampshire. His father served in the Revolution and was governor of the state

| Perry's visit to Japan

for a time. Franklin became a lawyer and a member of the state House of Representatives. He later served in both the House and the Senate in Washington. He also served without distinction as a general in the Mexican War. He was virtually unknown outside of New Hampshire when he was nominated for president in 1852.

Pierce was an easygoing man who tended to listen to the pro-Southern voices in his Cabinet. He was an expansionist, and his Southern friends specifically wanted lands suitable for the expansion of slavery. Pierce's foreign policy was a mixed bag, however, with a success that was not his doing and a failure that was.

The success came from Millard Fillmore. As president, Fillmore had dispatched Commodore Matthew Perry to the Far East to expand American trade in the Pacific. Perry carried a letter addressed to the ruler of Japan. Japan was at that time a completely closed society. It had refused to trade with the West, even imprisoning sailors shipwrecked on its shores. Perry, by a show of force with his modern gunboats, persuaded the Japanese to take his letter. Using tact and threats, Perry convinced the Japanese to open up their nation to trade with the United States. The treaty was approved by the Senate in 1854. It marked a turning point for Japan which changed from a medieval feudal kingdom to a world power in less than a hundred years.

Pierce's failure was an embarrassing attempt to add Cuba to the United States. Cuba, with its large slave-run sugar plantations, was a prize plum for the South as a way to add slave states to the Union. Pierce tried to purchase the island, but Spain absolutely refused. In 1854, Spanish officials seized an American steamer, the *Black Warrior*, in Cuba which triggered a crisis. The American ministers in Spain, Britain, and France were instructed to meet and draw up a plan for acquiring Cuba. The plan they drew up, the Ostend Manifesto, called for taking the island by force if Spain refused an offer of $120 million for it and if Spanish ownership endangered American interests.

The Ostend Manifesto became public and the reaction was wild. Northern abolitionists condemned the scheme as a blueprint for piracy. The publication of the secret plan was an acute embarrassment to the administration. Pierce dropped all attempts to take Cuba. The infighting over slavery had finally done what France, Britain, Mexico, and Spain could not do: halt the advance of Manifest Destiny.

Answer these questions.

3.67 What were the six major terms of the Compromise of 1850?

a. _____

b. _____

c. _____

d. _____

e. _____

f. _____

3.68 Where did the three old "giants" in the Congress stand on the Compromise?

Clay _____

Calhoun _____

Webster _____

3.69 How did the death of Zachary Taylor help the Compromise of 1850?

_____

_____

3.70 Why did the Southern states want Cuba?

_____

_____

3.71 What did Commodore Perry do that resulted in Japan becoming a world power?
_____
_____

3.72 What was the Ostend Manifesto and what happened when it became public?
_____
_____
_____

3.73 What was the Underground Railroad?
_____
_____
_____

Check the items that are true of the Fugitive Slave Act.

3.74 ☐ It hurt the abolitionist cause in the North.
3.75 ☐ An accused fugitive could post bail until his trial.
3.76 ☐ People helping enslaved people escape could be fined or imprisoned.
3.77 ☐ The commissioner got more money for returning a slave than he did for releasing a free man.
3.78 ☐ Northern mobs would sometimes free captured fugitives.
3.79 ☐ Franklin Pierce did not support it.
3.80 ☐ A captured black person could not testify in their own behalf.
3.81 ☐ Federal officials were required to act as slave catchers.
3.82 ☐ Harriet Tubman supported it.

A Growing Nation (1820–1855) | Unit 5

Uncle Tom's Cabin. The anti-slavery sentiment in the North received an incredible and unexpected boost in 1852. In that year, Harriet Beecher Stowe published the anti-slavery novel *Uncle Tom's Cabin*. Melding true stories taken from the files of the abolitionists, she wrote a compelling tale of a faithful slave named Tom. Tom was a committed Christian who obeyed his masters out of respect for God. He was sold twice in the novel, once to pay off a debt his master owed and another time when his master died. During his journeys he met other enslaved people and heard their heart-rending stories. The book also followed another slave named Eliza, who succeeded in fleeing to Canada when she was threatened with separation from her small son. Tom, in the meantime, was well-treated by his first two masters, but was beaten to death by the third, Simon Legree.

Uncle Tom's Cabin was one of the most successful pieces of **propaganda** in history. The phenomenal impact of the novel cannot be overstated. It sold hundreds of thousands of copies in the first year and millions thereafter. It was translated into several languages and became a popular stage play. It turned the nation against the evils of slavery. Lincoln reportedly said to Mrs. Stowe when they met in 1862, "So you're the little woman who wrote the book that made this great war."

The novel had a wide impact. It gave strength to the abolitionist cause and later to the Union in the Civil War. Its popularity in Britain made it difficult for that government to support the Confederacy. It spelled out in cold blood exactly what the North opposed. Southerners condemned it as an unfair and dishonest portrayal of slavery. However, they could not erase the image of faithful Tom dying of his wounds or desperate Eliza clutching her young child, racing across the ice floes of the Ohio River just a few yards ahead of the slave catchers.

Today, there are mixed reviews of the novel, some saying that the portrayal of the characters supports stereotyping and discrimination.

| A scene from *Uncle Tom's Cabin*

This doesn't change the fact that the story had the desired effect at that time period and impacted the views of many white people.

Kansas-Nebraska Act. The deaths of Clay, Calhoun, and Webster left the Senate in the control of lesser men. Dominant among these was the "Little Giant," Stephen Douglas, senator from Illinois. Douglas was a Democrat with no strong opinions on slavery. However, Illinois favored popular sovereignty. Douglas also had an eye on the presidency and needed Southern support to get it. Moreover, he had investments in Chicago and railroads. He wanted to organize the territories of the Midwest to allow a railroad to cross the center of the nation. Southern states opposed organizing those territories because they were north of the no-slavery line established by the Missouri Compromise and would become free states. Ignoring the problems he was about to create, Douglas found a way to get Southern support to organize the territories. In 1854 he dropped the bomb that undid the key compromises holding the nation together.

As the chairman of the Committee on Territories, Douglas proposed the Kansas-Nebraska Act to organize those territories. To gain the support of the South, the law would allow the people of the state to make decisions about slavery themselves. The carefully negotiated, long-standing Missouri Compromise was swept aside. Douglas used his influence and oratory skills to ram the law through Congress regardless of the consequences. Pliable Franklin Pierce signed it.

Northerners screamed in dismay. They felt betrayed. The carefully negotiated terms the North had accepted in 1820 had been dumped without compensation or agreement. Any territory might now become slave-holding, in spite of agreements to the contrary. The law turned even more Northerners against slavery because slaveholders could not be trusted to keep their bargains.

Douglas underestimated the reaction and results of his actions. He ended the era of compromise. The North steadfastly refused to enforce the Fugitive Slave Law now that the South was no longer honoring its agreements. That caused more bitterness in the South and more division in the nation. So, the Kansas-Nebraska Act doomed both the Missouri Compromise and the Compromise of 1850. The two sides no longer trusted each other enough to work out or keep delicate compromises.

Republican Party. The slavery issue had shattered the Whig party. It now created a new party. In 1854 the Republican Party was organized specifically opposing the spread of slavery. Spurred by the betrayal of the Kansas-Nebraska Act, the party gained strength quickly. The Republicans gathered up the remains of the northern Whig party, Know-Nothings, and supporters of free soil. They quickly became a national party, electing a Speaker of the House in 1856 and making a serious showing in the presidential election of that year.

The problem with the Republican Party was that it was clearly a Northern party. Until that time, the Whigs and the Democrats had support in both the North and the South. Thus, both parties had to compromise to please both parts of their membership. Unfortunately, the Kansas-Nebraska Act had broken the thin threads that held the parties together. The Democrats were also dividing on the slavery issue. They would present a united candidate in 1856, but in 1860 the Democratic Party would divide into Northern and Southern parts. Cooperation would yield to partisanship, which would yield to war.

| Stephen Douglas

Complete these sentences.

3.83 The anti-slavery novel _____ was one of the most successful pieces of propaganda in history.

3.84 The chief architect of the Kansas-Nebraska Act was _____ .

3.85 The _____ Party was organized to oppose the spread of slavery.

3.86 _____ was the author of *Uncle Tom's Cabin*.

3.87 The Republican Party was a party from the _____ section of the nation.

Put a *K* beside the items that were in whole or part a result of the Kansas-Nebraska Act.

3.88 _____ The rapid growth of the Republican Party

3.89 _____ The success of *Uncle Tom's Cabin*

3.90 _____ Popular sovereignty in Kansas and Nebraska

3.91 _____ The Missouri Compromise was overturned

3.92 _____ A new compromise was created

3.93 _____ Douglas acted heedlessly

3.94 _____ North-South distrust

3.95 _____ The Compromise of 1850 became stronger

3.96 _____ The Ostend Manifesto

Before you take this last Self Test, you may want to do one or more of these self checks.

1. _____ Read the objectives. See if you can do them.
2. _____ Restudy the material related to any objectives that you cannot do.
3. _____ Use the **SQ3R** study procedure to review the material:
    a. **S**can the sections.
    b. **Q**uestion yourself.
    c. **R**ead to answer your questions.
    d. **R**ecite the answers to yourself.
    e. **R**eview areas you did not understand.
4. _____ Review all vocabulary, activities, and Self Tests, writing a correct answer for every wrong answer.

SELF TEST 3

Choose the person who matches each item. Some answers will be used more than once (each answer, 2 points).

3.01	_____ Kansas-Nebraska Act	a. William Henry Harrison
3.02	_____ destroyed the National Bank	b. Eli Whitney
3.03	_____ cotton gin	c. Cyrus McCormick
3.04	_____ first textile factory in U.S.	d. Andrew Jackson
3.05	_____ telegraph	e. Joseph Smith
3.06	_____ steamboat	f. Henry Clay
3.07	_____ Erie Canal	g. Zachary Taylor
3.08	_____ Missouri Compromise	h. Stephen Douglas
3.09	_____ Buena Vista victory	i. Samuel Slater
3.010	_____ Mexico City victory	j. Commodore Matthew Perry
3.011	_____ interchangeable parts	k. Winfield Scott
3.012	_____ Mormon religion	l. Harriet Tubman
3.013	_____ over 300 slaves escaped to freedom	m. DeWitt Clinton
3.014	_____ treaty with Japan	n. Harriet Beecher Stowe
3.015	_____ Compromise of 1850	o. Samuel Morse
3.016	_____ *Uncle Tom's Cabin*	p. Robert Fulton
3.017	_____ the mechanical reaper	
3.018	_____ Father of the Factory System	
3.019	_____ "Log Cabin and Hard Cider"	
3.020	_____ Eaton scandal	
3.021	_____ became secretary of state due to a "corrupt bargain"	
3.022	_____ his death left Millard Fillmore as president	
3.023	_____ his followers founded the state of Utah	
3.024	_____ "Old Fuss and Feathers"	
3.025	_____ picked Martin Van Buren as his successor	

A Growing Nation (1820–1855) | Unit 5

Name the item described (each answer, 3 points).

3.026 _____ change from farming and handcrafting to industry and machine manufacturing

3.027 _____ secretive, anti-immigrant political party of the late 1840s

3.028 _____ Christian revival in 1790s to 1830s

3.029 _____ mission/fortress in Texas that was defended to the death by patriots, including Davy Crockett and Jim Bowie

3.030 _____ organization that helped slaves escape to Canada

3.031 _____ act that ended the Missouri Compromise and the era of compromises

3.032 _____ privately-owned toll roads that were the first improvements in American transportation

3.033 _____ the reason so many Irish came to America in 1845-1847

3.034 _____ the "Man-Stealing Law" that imprisoned people who helped slaves escape and denied recaptured slaves the right to a fair trial

3.035 _____ anti-slavery, Northern political party founded in 1854 that grew rapidly

Answer true or false (each answer, 1 point).

3.036 _____ Most factories were located in the Northeast because it had water power and a supply of capital.

3.037 _____ Factory workers were often shamefully exploited.

3.038 _____ Steamboats had little effect on the trade on the Mississippi River.

3.039 _____ Canals put the railroads out of business.

3.040 _____ Most of the immigrants in the 1840s and '50s came from Ireland, Britain, and France.

3.041 _____ Children were not employed in early factories.

3.042 _____ Mormons were persecuted because they practiced polygamy.

3.043 _____ Temperance was one of the reform movements of the mid-1800s.

3.044 _____ California became a state as part of the Missouri Compromise.

3.045 _____ The Ostend Manifesto was an anti-slavery document.

Unit 5 | **A Growing Nation (1820–1855)**

3.046 _____ Franklin Pierce wanted to add Cuba to the United States.

3.047 _____ Slavery was ended in Washington D.C. as part of the Compromise of 1850.

3.048 _____ Daniel Webster was a firm abolitionist, opposing the Compromise of 1850 because of his beliefs.

3.049 _____ The Wilmot Proviso would have forbidden slavery in the Mexican Cession.

3.050 _____ Manifest Destiny was the belief America would spread over the continent.

3.051 _____ John Tyler was a strong Whig, an admirer of Henry Clay.

3.052 _____ James Polk tried very hard to keep America out of a war with Mexico.

3.053 _____ John Quincy Adams supported the Gag Rule.

3.054 _____ Andrew Jackson successfully fought nullification.

3.055 _____ John Calhoun was a Southern leader.

3.056 _____ The Gadsden Treaty ended the Mexican War.

Before taking the LIFEPAC Test, you may want to do one or more of these self checks.

1. _____ Read the objectives. See if you can do them.
2. _____ Restudy the material related to any objectives that you cannot do.
3. _____ Use the **SQ3R** study procedure to review the material.
4. _____ Review activities, Self Tests, and LIFEPAC vocabulary words.
5. _____ Restudy areas of weakness indicated by the last Self Test.